D1553836

Rethinking Identity and Metaphysics

Rethinking Identity and Metaphysics

On the Foundations of Analytic Philosophy

Claire Ortiz Hill

Yale University Press   New Haven and London

Published with assistance from the Ernst Cassirer
Publications Fund.

Printed in the United States of America.

Library of Congress Cataloging-in-Publication Data
Hill, Claire Ortiz.
Rethinking identity and metaphysics : on the
foundations of analytic philosophy / Claire Ortiz Hill.
p.   cm.
Includes bibliographical references and index.
ISBN 0-300-06837-9 (cl : alk. paper)
1. Identity.   2. Metaphysics.   3. Frege, Gottlob,
1848–1925.   4. Russell, Bertrand, 1872–1970.
5. Marcus, Ruth Barcan.
I. Title.
BC199.I4H55   1997
111'.82—dc20   96-30387
                                          CIP

A catalogue record for this book is available from the
British Library.

The paper in this book meets the guidelines for
permanence and durability of the Committee on
Production Guidelines for Book Longevity of the
Council on Library Resources.

10   9   8   7   6   5   4   3   2   1

This book is dedicated to Fr. Henri Gauthier, O.F.M., cap.,
and the members of our Haitian community
in Washington, D.C.
When I was a stranger you welcomed me.

Thus there arises a queer twilight; the *equals* sign is treated in a half-and-half way, as known and again as unknown. . . . This twilight is needed by many mathematicians for the performance of their logical conjuring tricks. The ends that are meant to be achieved in this way are unexceptionably attained through our transformation of an equality that holds generally into an equality between graphs, by Axiom V (vol. 1, §3, §9, §20).

—Gottlob Frege, *The Basic Laws of Arithmetic*, vol. 2, §67.

Contents

ACKNOWLEDGMENTS

Gustave Flaubert once wrote that a writer should be like God in his universe, present in all parts but in none of them visible. I hope it will not distress the philosophers I wish to thank here if I say that they are divine in the way Flaubert describes. For it is an unfortunate fact of philosophical writing that the ideas of the philosophers one wishes most to thank are often present in all parts of one's work but in none of them visible because one's writings are filled with discussions of the ideas of those one is intent on refuting. An indication of this fact is that, despite appearances to the contrary, this book is about Edmund Husserl, though his name never appears in the body of the work. However, one has an opportunity to redress this injustice in the acknowledgments pages.

That veritable cornucopia of ideas Jaakko Hintikka lent me his ear during the time I was writing this book and was a cornucopia of encouragement. I cannot thank him enough for the generous way in which he provided me with moral support and practical help. The basic orientation of my philosophical work took shape while studying his work on intensional logic when I was writing my master's thesis at the Sorbonne on connections between Edmund Husserl's ideas, the logic of propositional attitudes, and possible worlds logic. All my work since has developed out of that thesis inspired by his work.

More visible in this book is Ruth Barcan Marcus, whom I first met in May 1986 when she came to Paris to receive the Medal of the Collège de France. Hearing her speak, I realized that we had come to many of the same conclusions from very different angles—she from her work investigating the contents of the referential opacity shelf, I from studying Husserl's criticisms of Frege's ideas on identity and how those ideas are connected with recent work in intensional logic. She and I talked at length. Her work is very rich, deep, and insightful, and I believe it will stand the test of time when the work of her contemporaries has bitten the dust. I've greatly appreciated her kind interest, encouragement, and help over the years. In 1891 Husserl wrote to Frege that of all the many writings he had before him as he worked on the *Philosophy of Arithmetic* he could not name another that he had studied with nearly as much enjoyment as he had Frege's *Foundations of Arithmetic*. He said he had derived constant pleasure from the originality of mind, clarity, and honesty of Frege's investigations, "which nowhere stretch a point or hold back a doubt, to which all vagueness in thought and word is alien, and which everywhere try to penetrate to the ultimate foundations." This is precisely how I felt while studying Marcus's *Modalities* as I worked on this book.

I also met Allan Casebier at the Collège de France that day. He deserves recognition for his work in founding the Society for the Study of Husserl's Philosophy, first conceived in the Café Rostand in Paris that May, which has done so much to bring together scholars working in the same area who were not working together. I have every reason to suspect that I owe him more than I realize.

Guillermo Rosado-Haddock and I began corresponding after I read his thesis on Husserl's philosophy of mathematics at the Husserl Archives in Leuven. He is an unusually good correspondent whose letters are filled with insightful ideas and suggestions. Working completely independently of each other in the late seventies, he and I came to many of the same conclusions about the Husserl-Frege relationship at a time when few (other than the French) would entertain the idea that Frege had not influenced Husserl. We in fact actually expressed our ideas using almost the same words. His ideas were published as "Remarks on Sense and Reference in Frege and Husserl" in *Kant Studien* 73, Heft 4, December 1982, 425–39.

Barry Smith has a way of appearing like a knight in shining armor brandishing his excellent critical skills just at the right time. He sat down in my armchair and read through and commented on this whole manuscript in one sitting, and with just two cups of tea. I am very grateful for the many ways in which he has helped me since we first met in 1977.

Invisible and yet present in all parts of this work are the various philosophers who have helped me over the years, and in particular, the teacher under whom I wrote my master's thesis and doctoral dissertation at the Sorbonne, Maurice Clavelin. He is invisibly present in all parts of my work because his influence on me has been a matter of form more than content. At the mere mention of Husserl's name he instantly looks pained, as if he were committing hari-kari. So I am particularly grateful that he agreed to harbor me, a Husserlian.

The links in the philosophical chain leading directly up to this book are Roger Schmidt, Bernd Magnus, Steve Erickson, Maurice Clavelin, David W. Smith, Fr. Tom Russman, and Fr. Jacques Sommet. When I was sixteen, Frank Blume suggested I take Roger Schmidt's philosophy course and arranged for me to do so. When I was nineteen, Bernd Magnus accepted to direct my senior honor's thesis on Husserl and in 1977 put me in touch with David W. Smith. And that set the ball in motion. But for Roger Schmidt, Maurice Clavelin, J. N. Mohanty, and (again) Maurice Clavelin, I would probably not be a philosopher. Quel noeud de vipères ont-ils mis bas!

I must also thank mathematicians Jean Petitot and Ivor Grattan-Guinness for their friendly encouragement. Philippe de Rouilhan deserves my gratitude for the truly chivalrous way in which he makes available to me the services and resources of the Institut d'Histoire et Philosophie des Sciences et des Techniques of University of Paris I. The librarians of the Institut Poincaré have also been very helpful.

In addition to the philosophers and mathematicians named above, over the years many scholars have sent me writings or made suggestions, sometimes very timely ones, that helped me with my research while I was writing this book. In this regard, I must thank Tyler Burge (UCLA), Christiane Chauviré (Paris), Francis Chilipaine (Malawi), Nino Cocchiarella (Indiana), Bob Cohen (Boston), Jairo da Silva (Sâo Paulo), Bratislav Fajkus (Prague), Solomon Fefermann (Stanford), Siegfried Gottwald (Leipzig), David Kaplan (UCLA), Lothar Kreiser (Leipzig), Gilbert Lelièvre (Paris), Tomasz Skura (Wroclaw), Judy Miles (Pomona), Kevin Mulligan (Geneva), Daniel Nicolet (Lausanne), Michael Picard (MIT), Francisco Rodriguez-Consuerga (Barcelona), Jan Sebestik (Paris), Jan Sjunnesson (Uppsala), Richard Tieszen (San Jose), Xavier Verley (Toulouse), Dallas Willard (USC).

Dr. Walter Emerson agreed to give me an engineer's opinion of the manuscript and surprised me by writing over sixteen pages of closely typed comments. He tells me that engineers have long been dealing in non-extensional notions and are better at it than philosophers.

I also want to thank Liesa Fox Nureyev for helping me establish the bibliography.

One after another my spiritual directors, Fr. Tom Russman (Capuchin), Fr. Jean Diot (Sulpician), and Fr. Jacques Sommet (Jesuit) have accompanied me in God's bright world. To them I owe my happiness. I am also deeply endebted to Fr. Jean-Marie Révillon who as the vicar for women religious of the archdiocese of Paris helped me arrange all the practical details of my life in Paris, which since 1984 have made it possible for me to carry on my work. I am also very grateful to my kind boss Sr. Monique Blondel (Little Sister of the Assumption) and I want to thank Madame Gilberte Beaux for her help, Harriet Blume for her early advice, and my friends for their fidelity.

Abbreviations

BY GOTTLOB FREGE

BL *The Basic Laws of Arithmetic.* Berkeley: University of California Press, 1964 (1893).

FA *The Foundations of Arithmetic.* Oxford: Blackwell, 1986 (1884), (2nd English ed. rev.).

GB *Translations from the Philosophical Writings of Gottlob Frege,* eds., P. Geach, and M. Black. Oxford: Blackwell, 1980, 3rd. ed.

PMC *Philosophical and Mathematical Correspondence.* Oxford: Blackwell, 1980.

PW *Posthumous Writings.* Oxford: Blackwell, 1979.

BY BERTRAND RUSSELL

EA *Essays on Analysis.* London: Allen & Unwin, 1973.

IMP *Introduction to Mathematical Philosophy.* London: Allen & Unwin, 1919.

LK *Logic and Knowledge.* London: Allen & Unwin, 1956.

PM *Principia Mathematica,* vol. 1. Cambridge: Cambridge University Press, 1927–28.

PofM *Principles of Mathematics.* London: Norton, 1903.

BY RUTH BARCAN MARCUS

M *Modalities.* New York: Oxford University Press, 1993.

BY WILLARD VAN ORMAN QUINE

FLPV   *From a Logical Point of View.* New York: Harper &
        Row, 1961 (1953).
OR   *Ontological Relativity and Other Essays.* New York:
        Columbia University Press, 1969.
WO   *Word and Object.* Cambridge, MA: M.I.T. Press,
        1960.
WP   *Ways of Paradox.* Cambridge, MA: Harvard
        University Press, 1976.

I

THE TWILIGHT ZONE

1

Unfettering Reasoning

Gottlob Frege wanted to break the domination of the word over the human mind by laying bare the misconceptions that arise through the use of ordinary language. As an essential part of this project he developed a symbolic language that he hoped would free thought from the fetters language imposed on it.[1]

In Frege's new symbolic language, nothing would be allowed to slip in unperceived into reasoning. All the principles appealed to would be set out in explicit terms, and precise transformation rules would show exactly what each step in the reasoning depended on. Frege even once confidently proclaimed that his symbolic language would not permit anything at all to slip in unnoticed into the reasoning that had not been expressly presupposed. Nor, he affirmed, would it "allow some other essential content from another source of knowledge to creep in unawares," even, he insisted, if this were something that seemed "so obvious that in ordinary thought we do not even notice that we are relying on it for support" (PMC, 100, 73).

Frege found an enthusiastic ally for his cause in Bertrand Russell, who hoped with the aid of symbolism to extend deductive reasoning to "regions of thought not usually supposed to be amenable to mathematical treatment" (PM, 3). Russell was quick to see how, by using a symbolic language, age-old philosophical problems could be made to seem to vanish with the stroke of a pen, and he even once went so far as to proclaim that "a good notation has a subtlety and suggestiveness which at times make it seem almost like a live teacher. Notational irregularities are often the first sign of philosophical errors," he wrote in his introduction to Wittgenstein's *Tractatus,* "and a perfect notation would be a substitute for thought."[2]

Through work connected with their efforts to develop symbolic logic, Frege and Russell managed to have a substantial impact on logic, philosophy, and mathematics in the twentieth century. However, in the late nineteenth century and the first decades of the twentieth century, mathematicians, logicians, and philosophers were forced to come to terms with some extremely difficult problems that are directly connected with Frege's and Russell's work in symbolic logic. The discovery of some of these problems—Russell's paradox or Gödel's incompleteness results, for example—had dramatic immediate consequences that shook the confidence that many, Russell and Frege among them, had had in techniques which had seemed so promising and were a source of undeniable progress in many areas. Other problems connected with these efforts, like the questions raised by the logic of propositional attitudes, certain questions involving identity, infinity, the continuum, modality, intensionality, and irrational numbers, still raise troublesome questions in spite of the rather considerable energy expended on them by some of the best minds of the twentieth century. In the following pages I take a close look at some of these undying problems associated with Frege's and Russell's symbolic languages by examining some really hard questions raised by the use of the equals sign in logic from Frege to the present day.

2

The Equals Sign

Even as Frege began to develop a formal language that he hoped could remove the ambiguity and imprecision imposed on reasoning by ordinary language, he was aware that the equals sign possessed an unusual property. Whereas in other contexts signs merely designate their content, he observed, "names at once appear *in propria persona* as soon as they are joined together by the symbol for equality of content." This, Frege reasoned in §8 of his 1879 *Begriffsschrift,* was because this particular sign expresses that two names have the same content, and "thus along with the introduction of the symbol for equality of content, all symbols are necessarily given a double meaning: the same symbols stand now for their own content, now for themselves" (GB, 10–12).

For Frege this particular kind of ambiguity introduced into reasoning by identity statements was not just a matter of signs or even just a matter of signs and what they stand for. A third crucial factor was involved: what Frege called "the way of determining the content." This could not be a matter of the symbolic expression alone, he contended, because the same content could be completely determined in different ways, and different names could be assigned to each of the ways in which it was determined. When this happened, and when two such signs designating the same content but determining it in different ways were linked to form a true identity statement, an informative statement could be the result. "The existence of different names for the same content," Frege averred in §8 of the *Begriffsschrift,* "is the very heart of the matter if each is associated with a different way of determining the content."

Frege was calling attention to the interesting fact that, taken at face value, statements of the form 'a = b' are plainly lies. They affirm the truth of something that is manifestly false. No two different names can ever be the same, thus any statement that affirms that they are cannot be true on the level of signs. However, it commonly happens that two different names refer to the same object, and when two such names are joined together by an identity sign an informative statement may be the result.[3]

In addition to the ambiguities inherent in identity statements that Frege noted in the *Begriffsschrift*, there is a fourth kind of ambiguity involved in the use of the equals sign in logical notation. This concerns the fact that the statement 'a = b' can be read either as 'a is equal to b', or 'a is identical to b'. According to dictionaries, two things are identical when they are the same in every way. They are equal when they are the same under a specific description, as given in a particular way. The difference between equality and identity would thus be the difference between sharing any given property or properties and having all properties in common.

Frege explicitly maintained and insisted throughout his writings[4] that in his logic there was no difference between equality and identity. "Whether we use 'the same' . . . or 'equal' is not of any importance. 'The same' may indeed be thought to refer to complete agreement in all respects, 'equal' only to agreement in this respect or that," he affirms in *Foundations of Arithmetic*, §65. By translating the sentences of ordinary language into his symbolic notation, though, he contended that the differences between equality and identity could be made to vanish, and he actually developed procedures by which he hoped one could transform statements about objects that are equal under a certain description into statements expressing complete identity.

In the following pages I closely examine significant logical and epistemological problems created when these ambiguities are allowed to slip into reasoning through the imperspicuous use of the identity sign. *The sign for identity is ambiguous and through it many a thing can creep into reasoning unnoticed.*

3

Confusing Sign and Object
in Identity Statements

"Identity," Willard Van Orman Quine wrote in his influential work *Word and Object*, "invites confusion between sign and object in men who would not make the confusion in other contexts" (WO, §24). And confusions brought on by the misleading bifurcation in meaning produced by the presence of the equals sign in canonical notation have indeed been a source of confusion and controversy for those who have sought to further the work Frege began. Moreover, it is clear that logicians cannot afford to overlook such difficulties because the preeminent role identity statements have been assigned in symbolic logic means that deeper issues certainly lurk behind what might be considered to be a relatively superficial matter of cleaning up argumentation by perspicuously distinguishing between the mention and use of signs.

For example, the logical behavior of identity statements became a major issue in the decades-long controversy between Quine and modal logicians when Quine tried to dismiss modern modal logic as illegitimate because he thought, as Ruth Barcan Marcus put it, it was conceived in the sin of confusing use and mention (M, 5). Quine's attempt to discredit modal logic by linking it with confusions of mention and use (WP, 177-79) stimulated a debate (discussed in chapter 11) that widened into a controversy concerning the existence, nature, and import of the confusions Quine found so distressing. These discussions have raised profound questions about the very nature of the logical enterprise as redefined by Frege, Russell, and their successors, and so sustained Frege's conviction that "different names for the same content are not always just a trivial matter of formulation; if they go along with different ways of determining the content, they are relevant to the essential nature of the case" (GB, 12). Before looking at the deeper issues at stake, however, we need to take a close look at what is at stake in the seemingly simple task of distinguishing between names and what they name.

Some Sources of the Trouble

One source of the trouble, Quine explained in *Mathematical Logic,* §4, is "forgetting that a statement about an object must contain a name of the object rather than the object itself. If the object is a man or a city, physical circumstances prevent the error of using it instead of its name; when the object is a name or other expression in turn, the error is easily committed."[5] This ambiguity that is embedded into language by its very nature easily slips into reasoning through the identity statements of symbolic logic because, as Frege was insightful enough to see right from the very beginning, names connected by the sign for identity have the unusual property of sometimes standing for themselves and sometimes for their objects (GB, 11).

The apparently simple task of distinguishing an object and the way it is named can become an exceedingly difficult job once the mind enters the abstract realms of thought made accessible to it by symbolic reasoning. There even the most concrete objects become intangible when marks on a piece of paper are made to stand for them. For even the most real and palpable qualities of material things vanish when symbols take their places in abstract arguments, and the senses face nothing more than written characters. Though a hungry person can easily distinguish a steak from the word designating it on a menu, once one leaves the familiar world of everyday things for the considerably less material worlds that are mapped out in logical or mathematical notation, symbols can easily begin to seem to be the things themselves in the minds of those carrying out the reasoning and of those persuaded by their arguments.

The problem becomes all the more acute in reasoning carried out in purely theoretical fields where the objects dealt with—sets or classes, for example—often have no material existence at all, and so are far more abstract in nature than steaks in restaurants are. In the introduction to *Principia Mathematica*, Russell eloquently describes the process that symbolic logic is meant to facilitate in a way which illustrates the precise trap that lies in wait for those venturing into abstract realms of thought:

> The adaptation of the rules of the symbolism to the processes of deduction aids the intuition in regions too abstract for the imagination readily to present to the mind the true relation between the ideas employed. For various collocations of symbols become familiar as representing important collocations of ideas; and in turn the possible relations—according to the rules of symbolism—between these collocations of symbols become familiar, and these further collocations represent still more complicated relations between abstract ideas. And thus the mind is finally led to construct trains of reasoning in regions of thought in which the imagination would be entirely unable to sustain itself without symbolic help (PM, 2).

DISTINGUISHING THE NAME FROM THE NAMED

"If a conqueror burns a city," Frege reminded us in *Basic Laws II*, "he does not burn the name of the city; what happens to a thing does not automatically happen to its sign" (GB, 177).

Perfectly conscious of the ambiguity inherent in identity state-ments, Frege himself always scrupulously distinguished between names and their objects by placing quotation marks around the expressions he used to designate the names themselves. In *Basic Laws I,* he defended his frequent use of quotation marks against charges of pedantry noting that "an inexact mode of speak-ing or writing, which perhaps was originally employed only for greater convenience or brevity and with full consciousness of its inaccuracy, may end in a confusion of thought when once that consciousness has disappeared" (BL, §0).

And Frege's fears were confirmed as his admonitions went unheeded by those who first transmitted his insights to the English speaking world. Bertrand Russell was initially blind to the problem and so fell right into the trap symbolic languages lay. His main works are replete with the error Frege was so de-termined to avoid, and through them confusions of use and mention passed unperceived into logical reasoning.

For instance Russell once went so far as to insist in a letter to Frege that "in spite of all its snowfields Mont Blanc itself is a component part of what is actually asserted in the proposi-tion 'Mont Blanc is more than 4000 metres high'" (PMC, 169). Frege spotted Russell's errors, once confessing in a letter to Jour-dain that he never knew for sure whether Russell was speaking of a sign or its content (PMC, 78, 84). Russell did eventually take note of the problem, and in 1918 it was a chastened man who spoke of the importance of theory of symbolism for phi-losophy, which, he said:

> lies in the fact that unless you are fairly self-conscious about symbols, unless you are fairly aware of the relation of the symbol to what it symbol-izes, you will find yourself attributing to the thing properties which only belong to the symbol. That,

of course, is especially likely in very abstract studies such as philosophical logic, because the subject-matter that you are supposed to be thinking of is so exceedingly difficult and elusive that any person who has ever tried to think about it knows you do not think about it except perhaps once in six months for half a minute. The rest of the time you think about the symbols, because they are tangible, but the thing you are supposed to be thinking about is fearfully difficult and one does not often manage to think about it (LK, 185).

In his doctoral dissertation Quine set out to "clean up" the confusions of use and mention present in Russell's *Principia Mathematica*[6] and has been tireless in his efforts to eradicate them from logical reasoning altogether. As a step in his sustained effort to stem the tide of "confusion and controversy" resulting from failures to distinguish clearly between an object and its name, Quine illustrated the differences between names and what they name by using the following short exercise to spell out some of differences:

'Boston is populous' is about Boston and contains 'Boston'; ''Boston' is disyllabic' is about 'Boston' and contains ''Boston''. ''Boston'' designates 'Boston', which in turn designates Boston. To mention Boston we use 'Boston' or a synonym, and to mention 'Boston' we use ''Boston'' or a synonym. ''Boston'' contains six letters and just one pair of quotation marks; 'Boston' contains six letters and no quotation marks; and Boston contains some 800,000 people.[7]

The Principle of Substitutivity of Identicals
and Failures of Substitutivity

Given a true statement of identity, standard logical wisdom tells us, then one of its terms can be substituted for the other in any true statement and the result will be true. This is known as the principle of substitutivity of identicals. It is often associated with Leibniz's principle of substitutivity according to which "Things are the same as each other of which one can be substituted for the other salva veritate." If x and y are identical, it is reasoned, then y has every property x does. So everything that can be said of the one can, then, be said of the other. Therefore they are interchangeable, or so it would seem.[8]

Supposing this interchangeability to be the case, the principle of substitutivity could then act as a sort of lie detector test with failures of substitutivity serving to indicate that false identification has been made and revealing that one has attempted to interchange things that on the surface appear to be the same but which further analysis may prove not to be so. Or such failures could reveal that one has made the more subtle error of identifying things that actually belong to different logical types. Failures of substitutivity can also serve as indicators that certain logical phenomena that many philosophers thought they were successfully exorcising actually remain in their argumentation and do not vanish with the stroke of a pen.

It is very easy to find cases in which substitutivity fails. For instance, basic differences between names and objects stand out in identity statements in which use and mention have been confused. Though such statements may pass many tests, and although in symbolic discourse the differences between signs and objects can often be so subtle as to appear non-existent or harmless, failure of substitutivity shows that words standing for names and words standing for objects cannot be interchanged with impunity. For as Ruth Barcan Marcus has pointed out, identity is a clear guide to ontology. "That there are individuals is already presupposed if the identity relation is to hold. . . . Identity is an essential feature of things . . . no identity without entity" (M, 200).

The following simple example reveals a bit how identity can limn the central traits of reality by indicating that we have mixed our objects with something else. Given the following true statements:

(1) Certain things that Richard Nixon did during his political career earned him the name Tricky Dick.

(2) Richard Nixon = Tricky Dick

By interchanging the words appearing on either side of the equals sign in (2) we obtain the obviously false statement:

(3) Certain things that Richard Nixon did during his political career earned him the name Richard Nixon.

Something obviously has gone wrong. Nixon never did anything during his political career to earn him the name his parents gave him at birth.

We have unthinkingly confused a name with a person, something that an appeal to our quotation device could have spared us. For by using it we might have readily seen we were asking for trouble by identifying a flesh and blood person with a set of letters forming a particular unflattering name by which he had been known, by assuming that:

(4) Richard Nixon = 'Tricky Dick'

Likewise, the falsehood of:

(5) 'Richard Nixon' = 'Tricky Dick'

becomes clear once one examines the countless number of false statements that can be produced by interchanging the names appearing on either side of the equals sign. In this case substitution would turn a true statement like:

(6) Richard Nixon signed 'Richard Nixon' to important government documents.

into the obvious falsehood:

(7) Richard Nixon signed 'Tricky Dick' to important government documents.

Nixon surely never signed the mean nickname 'Tricky Dick' to any government documents. Here substitution has failed, as well it should. Statements that, either explicitly or implicitly, equate two names, or equate a name and an object are lies, and failures of substitution are one proof of that.

So the principle of substitutivity of identicals must be amended in a way that accounts for the fact that names and objects possess different properties; it must be clearly stipulated that, in spite of any appearances to the contrary, in true statements of the form 'x = y', it is not 'x' and 'y' themselves that are declared to be the same, rather 'x' and 'y' are said to refer to the same object, and by virtue of this should be interchangeable everywhere salva veritate.

The amendment is needed because what can be said of a name will not also be true of what it names, and vice versa. Confusion and seemingly paradoxical consequences can result, and have resulted, when the word standing for a name and the word standing for the object which that name names are mistakenly interchanged. When allowed to slip unnoticed into reasoning this may have unexpected, disturbing, and misleading effects. Such confusions, I argue, have been even a greater source of pseudoproblems in philosophy than has yet been imagined.

Ever conscious of potential traps set by confusions of use and mention, Quine was careful to define identity in *Word and Object*, §24, as what "is expressed in English by those uses of 'is' that one is prepared to expand into 'is the same object as'. . . . The sign '=' of identity . . . joins singular terms to make a sentence. The sentence thus formed is true if and only if those component terms refer to the same object." That being so, basic intuitions concerning words and the things to which they refer are confirmed as is evident in the true inference:

(8) Tricky Dick's collaborators engaged in a dirty tricks campaign.
(9) Tricky Dick is the same man as Richard Nixon.
(10) Therefore, Richard Nixon's collaborators engaged in a dirty tricks campaign.

The names figuring in these statements are "purely referential," and thus subject to the principle of substitutivity of identity. What is true of Tricky Dick here is true of him regardless of the fact that we have referred to him in a different way in (10). The important thing is that the names name the same man and that the historical facts sanction what has been predicated of him. So (9) being true, we are justified by substitution in deriving (10) from (8). No confusions of use and mention have intervened here to interrupt the referential force of the names that refer to their objects transparently, not in the opaque way that makes substitutivity fail. Any number of like examples can be produced in which any objections made to the substitution, or to any inference made owing to it, can be readily dismissed as being merely linguistic, subjective, or inconsequential in nature (W&O, §30).

OPACITY AND QUANTIFICATION

The kind of irreferentiality present where use and mention have been confused also threatens another basic principle of inference: existential generalization. For many philosophers the objects referred to in a theory are not the things the singular terms name. They are the values of the variables of quantification.[9] Thus, it is essential for these philosophers to be able to move from a statement in which something is affirmed of an object to a quantified statement that affirms that there is an object x such that. . . . This move is licensed by the principle of existential generalization.

Since the basic idea underlying this theory of quantification is "that whatever is true of the object named by a given singular term is true of something," existential generalization clearly loses its justification when the singular term to be quantified over fails to name (FLPV, 145). Since a singular term that fails to name cannot meaningfully figure in an identity statement either, substitutivity—that arch indicator of referential transparency—and existential generalization work hand in hand to license inference between sentences. Together they make up a basic part of the deductive apparatus that yields logical truths. Referential opacity is, then, doubly heinous because it brings two prime principles of inference to grief.

As part of his lifelong campaign to drive referential opacity out of logic, Quine has issued repeated warnings about the dangers posed by the kind of irreferentiality associated with confusions of mention and use. His particular concern is intimately linked with his idea that existential quantifiers are on a distinct ontological mission. For him:

> The objects whose existence is implied in our discourse are finally just the objects which must, for the truth of our assertions, be acknowledged as "values of variables", i.e., be reckoned into the totality of objects over which our variables of quantification range. To be is to be a value of a variable.

> There are no ultimate philosophical questions concerning terms and their references, but only concerning variables and their values; and there are no ultimate philosophical problems concerning existence except insofar as existence is expressed by the quantifier '$(\exists x)$'.[10]

Referential opacity mars the beauty of this kind of quantification theory, but the problems are not just skin deep and do not go away once surface confusions are weeded out of reasoning. Substitutivity and existential generalization also encounter obstacles in a wide variety of epistemic, doxastic, causal, deontic, and modal contexts that are found all the time in and out of philosophical, scientific, medical, and legal discourse. Something resembling referential opacity can be spotted in propositional attitude contexts and within the range of modal operators. There it raises far deeper questions for philosophers than does the referential opacity associated with bona fide confusions of mention and use—which after all are relatively easy to wipe out.

Scientific theories teem with singular terms that fail to denote even though philosophers like Quine cannot quantify into the constructions involved. For instance, is AIDS research to halt because there does not now exist, and possibly never will exist, an x such that x cures AIDS? Was it unscientific to look for a virus that causes AIDS at a time when it was only possible that there was an x such that x was a virus that caused AIDS?

Fortunately, not all philosophers have been so squeamish about superficial unclarity, nor so loath as Quine to take a close look at what precisely might be swimming in the opaque puddle of irreferentiality. Rather than flee any hint of referential opacity as Quine has advised (WO, chap. 6), or just stand by and watch fundamental principles of inference fail, philosophers like Jaakko Hintikka and Ruth Barcan Marcus have seen through the surface messiness to deeper problems. They have sought to explore what Quine would dispose of, developing intensional languages powerful enough to make up for the shortcomings of Quine's sort of logic and striving to achieve clarity where at first blush there seemed to be none.

Confusing Names and Descriptions in Identity Statements

"One feature of language that threatens to undermine the reliability of thinking," Gottlob Frege wrote in the last year of
his life, "is its tendency to form proper names to which no objects correspond" (PW, 269). The presence of the definite article
in a phrase, he explained, can create the impression that the
phrase designates an object, and so the phrase may come to be
in a place for which it is unsuited. "The difficulties which this
idiosyncrasy of language entangles us in are incalculable," he
warned, and he came to rue that he had let himself be tricked by
what he called the "fatal tendency of language to form apparent proper names" (PW, 270). Frege actually saw a connection
between such expressions containing the definite article and the
contradictions, or paradoxes, connected with set theory, and so
he finally blamed such confusions for the failure of his attempt
to place number theory on scientific foundations (PW, 269–70;
PMC, 55).

Bertrand Russell inherited Frege's logical woes, and so he too
was compelled to come to terms with certain difficult questions
raised by the name-like behavior of expressions of the form 'the
so and so' which, on the surface, seem to denote objects directly
and often figure in identity statements as if they do. Russell
would even go so far as to write in his *Introduction to Mathematical Philosophy* that he considered analyses of the word 'the'
to be of so very great importance to a correct understanding
of descriptions and classes that he would give the doctrine of

the word if he were dead from the waist down and not merely in prison (where he was at the time) (IMP, 167). He, too, saw a connection between the logical behavior of descriptions and the paradoxes of set theory.[11] His famous theory of definite descriptions played an important role in his efforts to eliminate problems that defeated Frege.

In the latter half of the twentieth century, confusions about the logical behavior of descriptions again made their way into major philosophical discussions when Quine accorded them a central place in his campaign against modal and intensional logics. So confusions about reference and descriptions have played a significant role in twentieth-century philosophy, and, as I argue throughout this book, a greater role has yet to be recognized because the links between them and certain other sorrows besetting philosophers have yet to be established in a way that brings the deepest underlying issues to the surface.

FREGE ON IDENTIFYING NAMES AND DESCRIPTIONS

In Frege's logic, descriptions like 'the discoverer of America', 'the number of Jupiter's moons', or 'the extension of the word 'star'' were treated as referring to self-subsistent objects, and as such were apt to figure in identity statements. Early in his attempts to provide sound logical foundations for numbers, he wrote in *Foundations of Arithmetic* that in the case of 'the number of Jupiter's moons is four':

> The word "is" should not be taken as a mere copula, as in the proposition "the sky is blue". This is shown by the fact that we can say: "the number of Jupiter's moons is the number four, or 4". Here "is" has the sense of "is identical with" or "is the same as". So what we have is an identity, stating that the expres-

sion "the number of Jupiter's moons' signifies the same object as the word "four" (FA, §57).

He concludes this passage affirming that "it is the same man that we call Columbus and the discoverer of America."

In a 1919 letter to Paul Linke, Frege discussed the matter more thoroughly:

> An object can be designated either by a proper name or by a sign—e.g., 'the victor of Austerlitz'—which can stand for a proper name (individual name). An individual name is formed out of a *nomen appellativum* by adding the definite article or a demonstrative pronoun to it. But properly speaking this is permissible only if the concept of the *nomen appellativum* is not empty and if only one object falls under it.... In the proposition 'Napoleon is loser of Waterloo' we have the sense of subsumption; in the proposition 'Napoleon is the loser of Waterloo' we have an equation. The left designatum is the same as the right designatum, just as in the proposition 'the loser of Waterloo is the victor of Austerlitz, or as in the proposition '$7 + 5$ is 6.2'.... The proposition 'Napoleon is the loser of Waterloo' can be changed into 'Napoleon is identical with the loser of Waterloo' (PMC, 96, 98).

However, it was precisely this "idiosyncrasy," this "fatal tendency of language to form apparent proper names," which he finally concluded had entangled him "in incalculable difficulties." And he blamed a particular case of this error for having led to the paradoxes of set theory that he came to believe had made set theory impossible: "A particularly noteworthy example of this is the formation of a proper name after the pattern of 'the extension of the concept a', e.g. 'the extension of the concept *star*'. Because of the definite article, this expression appears to designate an object; but there is no object for which this phrase could be a linguistically appropriate designation. From this has arisen the paradoxes of set theory which have dealt the death blow to set theory itself" (PW, 269). Since Russell found himself forced to contend with the puzzles and paradoxes connected with Frege's logic, it is not surprising that he tangled with the problem Frege described above.

Russell on Names, Descriptions, and Identity

Like Frege, Russell originally considered statements equating a term standing for an object with a description to be identities, and identities to be statements that equated objects. Russell originally believed that all expressions denote directly that, "if a word means something, there must be some thing that it means."[12] But his struggle to solve the paradoxes forced him to come to terms with serious logical problems that seemed to him unavoidable when definite descriptions are regarded as standing for genuine constituents of the propositions in which they figure.

One of the most significant puzzles associated with descriptions containing the definite article Russell confronted is directly tied in with Leibniz's principle of the substitutivity of identicals. If identity can only hold between 'x' and 'y' if they are different symbols for the same object, Russell reasoned, it would not then seem to have much importance. However, he observed, identity statements containing descriptive phrases of the form 'the so-and-so' constitute an exception to this and so lead to a puzzle. He explained:

> If *a* is identical with *b*, whatever is true of the one is true of the other, and either may be sub-

stituted for the other in any proposition without altering the truth or falsehood of that proposition. Now George IV wished to know whether Scott was the author of *Waverley;* and in fact Scott *was* the author of *Waverley.* Hence we may substitute *Scott* for *the author of 'Waverley',* and thereby prove that George IV wished to know whether Scott was Scott. Yet an interest in the law of identity can hardly be attributed to the first gentleman of Europe (LK, 47–48).

If the expression 'the author of *Waverley*' really does denote some object c, Russell finally reasoned, the proposition 'Scott is the author of *Waverley*' would be of the form 'Scott is c'. But if 'c' denoted any one other than Scott, this proposition would be false; while if 'c' denoted Scott, the resulting proposition would be 'Scott is Scott', which is self-evident, trivial, and plainly different from 'Scott is the author of *Waverley*', which may be true or false. So, Russell concluded, 'c' does not stand simply for Scott, nor for anything else (PM, 67; LK, 245–48) because:

No one outside a logic-book ever wishes to say '*x* is *x*', and yet assertions of identity are often made in such forms as 'Scott was the author of *Waverley*'. . . . The meaning of such propositions cannot be stated without the notion of identity, although they are not simply statements that Scott is identical with another term, the author of *Waverley.* . . . The shortest statement of 'Scott is the author of *Waverley*' seems to be 'Scott wrote *Waverley;* and it is always true of *y* that if *y* wrote *Waverley,* *y* is identical with Scott' (LK, 55).

According to this analysis, the description may be substituted for 'y' in any propositional function fy and a significant proposition will be the result. The truth value of many of the propositions we commonly make about the so-and-so remains unchanged when 'y' is substituted for 'the so-and-so'.[13] These reflections on substitutivity and definite descriptions led Russell to the conclusion that all phrases (other than propositions) containing the word 'the' (in the singular) are incomplete symbols that have a meaning in use but when taken out of context do not actually denote anything at all (PM, 67–68). He explained:

> The reason why it is imperative to analyse away the phrase, 'the author of Waverley may be stated as follows. It is plain that where we say 'the author of Waverley is the author of Marmion', the *is* expresses identity. We have seen also that the common *denotation*, namely Scott, is not a constituent of this proposition, while the *meanings* (if any) of 'the author of Waverley' and 'the author of Marmion' are not identical. . . . 'The author of Waverley' . . . would have to be what was said to be identical with the *meaning* of 'the author of Marmion'. This is plainly not the case; and the only escape is to say that 'the author of Waverley does not, by itself, have a meaning, though phrases of which it is a part do have a meaning. That is, in a right analysis of the above proposition, 'the author of Waverley' must disappear. This is effected when the above proposition is analysed as meaning: 'Some one wrote Waverley, and no one else did, and that someone else wrote Marmion and no one else did.'[14]

Russell considered this theory of definite descriptions to have been his most valuable contribution to philosophy and frequently spoke in enthusiastic terms of its role in resolving his logical problems, and the paradoxes associated with set theory in particular.[15] He once claimed that his success in his article "On Denoting," where he first expounded it, was the source of all his subsequent progress. As a consequence of his new theory of denoting, he said, he found at last that substitution would work, and all went swimmingly.[16] This new theory, he claimed, "swept away a host of otherwise insoluble problems."[17]

OPACITY AND DESCRIPTIONS

To shed light on some of the issues underlying problems and puzzles that have haunted logical arguments that use statements in which names are identified with descriptions, I now take a closer look at Frege's examples of such statements as they relate to Quine's theories about referential opacity and the substitutivity of identity.

In his 1884 *Foundations of Arithmetic*, §57, Frege appealed to this bit of nineteenth-century schoolchild wisdom to illustrate his point about identity:

(1) 'The number of Jupiter's moons is the number 4'.

Here, Frege contended, the 'is' is the is of identity; it is equivalent to writing 'is the same as'. 'The number of Jupiter's moons' signifies the same object as the word 'four'. In order to determine just what manner of expression the description figuring in (1) may actually be, I submit it to Quine's criterion of the substitutivity of identity. If the description figuring there really does name an object, then Frege's statement should stand the substitutivity test in standard extensional contexts.

Now according to Quine's ideas about identity, substitutivity, opacity and quantification, a statement like Frege's (1) would have the logical form of a identity. According to both men, the expressions being equated designate objects. And as long as 4 is the same number as the number as Jupiter's moons, one may substitute one side of the equation for the other in all contexts or any and a true statement will result.[18]

(1) The number of Jupiter's moons is the number 4.
(2) 4 is less than 5.
(3) Therefore, the number of Jupiter's moons is less than 5.

The inference made does not on the surface appear to be illegitimate. Granting that the number of Jupiter's moons is indeed the number 4 (which apparently was true for Frege in 1884), then (3) seems to validly follow from (1) and (2) by substitution based on the identity.

Only on further investigation do the problems come to the surface. Only then do we see that (3) is a product of an illicit union performed in (1); it was conceived in the sin of confusing descriptions and objects. For the description 'the number of Jupiter's moons' does not designate any particular object and so cannot an identity make. It designates a single, inessential property of the number 4, and one that number sloughed off the instant astronomers discovered that the number of Jupiter's moons was rather greater than 4.

Even were we to change Frege's example to the more comfortable:

(4) 'The number of Jupiter's moons is 12'.

the description 'the number of Jupiter's moons' would not be intersubstitutable with '12' in very many contexts because the number 12 has any number of properties which the number of Jupiter's moons does not and cannot have. In this particular case, 12 has never been 4. The numbers 12 and 4 are e'er fixed marks in ways which the number of Jupiter's moons are not and cannot be. Although Frege thought (1) was true in 1884, the number of Jupiter's moons has been discovered by astronomers to be at least 12, but 4 has not been discovered to be 12, so (3) would have the opposite truth value for Frege in 1884 than it would have for Quine one hundred years later.

Although neither the actual number of Jupiter's moons, nor the number 4 has changed, Quine's reading of 'the number of Jupiter's moons' would not be identical to Frege's. It is the fundamental irreferentiality of descriptions that is behind the untoward behavior manifested in the inference.

In his 1919 letter to Linke, Frege also provided these examples of what he considered to be true identities (PMC, 96, 98):

(8) 'Napoleon is the loser of Waterloo'.
(9) 'The loser of Waterloo is the victor of Austerlitz'.

In each one of these cases the left designatum is the same as the right designatum, he avers. The proposition 'Napoleon is the loser of Waterloo' can be changed into 'Napoleon is identical with the loser of Waterloo', he affirms.

However, a description, even a definite description, can never be the same as what it describes. A description only gives a particular property of its reference or would-be reference. But objects are infested with properties and so can be determined in innumerably different ways. And when the very same reference is given in a different way, there is no guarantee that it will be recognizable as the same object that is being determined in different ways. For example, how many people will recognize Napoleon as the second son of Letizia Ramolino or the victor of Lodi?

The same object can also be uniquely described in very heterogeneous ways, and so substitution in perfectly extensional contexts may produce completely nonsensical results. Although equivalent, these descriptions will not necessarily be interchangeable salva veritate, as the failures of substitutivity arise out of the mistaken assumption that descriptive phrases can exhibit the same logical behavior as objects. If (8) and (9) actually were true identities then everything that is true of the loser of Waterloo would be true of the victor of Austerlitz, and vice versa. Consequently, by appealing to Leibniz's law we might easily obtain:

(10) The loser of Waterloo went on to other victories.
(11) The victor of Austerlitz was a defeated man.

For Napoleon's defeats are surely just as indissolubly glued to him as are his victories.

Descriptions are intensional, not extensional in nature. Like Frege's senses, they serve to illuminate only a single aspect of the thing meant; they give their reference incompletely (GB, 58). It is this merely partial illumination that gives rise to the phenomenon of opacity that has annoyed Quine and others, and it does so even in normally extensional contexts. Whereas a definite description of an object may alone suffice to fix the object of reference uniquely, no single description, no matter how definite, will ever suffice to characterize the reference adequately enough to bar any other descriptions ostensibly identifiable with the same object which could turn up to upset inference and change our truths into falsehoods, or give truth to a lie.

Russell was lucid about the problem. "There is no backward road from denotations to meanings, because every object can be denoted by an infinite number of different denoting phrases" (LK, 50), he explained to readers of "On Denoting" as he gave his theory of definite descriptions for the first time. In other words although all roads may lead to Rome, only one will take you back by the way you came. Although all your descriptions may lead *to* the very same reference, only one can ever take you back to that particular description by the way you came.

Russell did his best to make the one-way street into the two-way street of identity that the principles of substitutivity of identity and existential generalization require, that is, to make an irreversible relation into a reversible one via his theory of definite descriptions.

5

Confusing Concepts and Objects in Identity Statements

Confusion and controversy have also resulted from failure to distinguish between objects and intensional phenomena such as concepts, senses, attributes, properties, and essences that often find their way into identity statements. And here the problems are much more subtle and harder to uncover and correct than are confusions of mention and use in identity statements. In this chapter I present some initial arguments as to why concepts are not to be identified with objects; in later chapters I discuss some special problems arising from confusing concepts and other intensional phenomena with objects or signs. By showing how, from a logical point of view, intensions differ from objects and signs, I will demonstrate that they are not to be dismissed as psychological phenomena. I argue that the efforts of logicians who have fought to eliminate intensions have served only to demonstrate the reality and ineradicability of the phenomena they have wanted to ban. For intensions have vigorously resisted analyses that do not take certain logical, ontological, linguistic, and grammatical differences obtaining between them and objects into account. And I will therefore illustrate the extent to which experience has now shown the futility and error of engaging in logical analyses that play on confusions of objects and intensions, or try to dissolve, eclipse, annihilate, stifle, cloak, disregard, or ban differences obtaining between them.

One source of the trouble is the fact that a given object, a concept associated with it, and a word used to describe it are often found wearing the same linguistic dress. For example, a word like 'dinosaur' stands for itself and designates both each dinosaur that has ever existed and the concept dinosaur that contains the properties something must have to be called a dinosaur. Even when one is being very scrupulous, the differences between words, objects, and concepts designated by the same expressions can become maddeningly elusive in certain contexts, thereby generating baffling and disturbing logical anomalies when, for instance, a word designating a concept becomes confused with the objects the same word refers to.

The problem is additionally hard to tackle because so many philosophers in this century have wanted to get rid of intensions entirely and to deny them any objective existence. So they have intentionally and unrepentingly identified intensions with objects because the latter docilely submit to substitution and so are more amenable to the extensional treatment. When intensions have defied translation into terms classical logic can handle, they have often been dismissed as psychological in origin or confused with their linguistic expression. The latter is a special case of a confusion between use and mention because, if it can be shown (1) that intensions enjoy an objective existence independent of the signs used to express them in language or individual mental states, and (2) that intensions rebel when subjected to the same logical rules objects obey, then it would be a grievous logical sin to yield to the temptation to dismiss them as psychological or to try to identify them with objects or treat them as signs.

The Logical Characteristics of Concepts According to Frege

Although many philosophers emphasize the abstract or ideal qualities of concepts and other intensions, Gottlob Frege principally defined concepts in terms of some very tangible logical properties. "The essence of concepts," he wrote in 1900, "can be characterized by saying that they have a predicative nature" (PMC, 92). A concept, he wrote over and over again, "is predicative. It is the reference of a grammatical predicate; the name of an object is quite incapable of being used as a grammatical predicate."[19]

According to Frege, the predicable nature of concepts is conferred on them by a particular kind of incompleteness and dependency that they exhibit with regard to objects. For Frege, concepts stand in need of supplementation and of completion, and he always cited this fundamentally incomplete nature of concepts as constituting the principal difference between them and objects. In Frege's special vocabulary, "a concept is unsaturated in that it requires something to fall under it; hence it cannot exist on its own" (PMC, 101). A concept word "contains a gap which is intended to receive a proper name" (PMC, 55). It makes no sense to try to fit together the two complete parts, Frege reasoned. At least one of them must be unsaturated or predicative; otherwise they would not hold together (GB, 24, 25, 31, 46–48, 50, 54; PMC, 101, 141; PW, 119–20).

The essential differences between concepts and objects are, though, Frege recognized, "covered up in our word languages" (PMC, 55) where "the two merge into each other" (PMC, 100), and "the sharpness of the difference is somewhat blurred, in that what were originally proper names (e.g., 'moon'), can become concept words, and what were originally concept words (e.g., 'God') can become proper names" (PMC, 92); "the proper name 'sun' becomes a concept name when one speaks of suns, and a concept name with a demonstrative serves to designate an individual" (PMC, 100).

However, Frege warned, "we must not let ourselves be deceived because language often uses the same word now as a proper name, now as a concept-word" (GB, 50). And in order to help stem the tide of confusion and controversy that can arise when a concept appears wearing the same linguistic dress as an object or a word or when it appears in the subject position in a sentence, Frege advised adopting a special convention by which one might scrupulously distinguish words referring to concepts from words naming objects or names in logical discussions in which concepts, objects, and words might become confused (GB, 46). He gave this example to illustrate some of the differences:

> Confusion easily arises . . . through our not making a sufficient distinction between concept and object. If we say: 'A square is a rectangle in which the adjacent sides are equal,' we define the concept *square* by specifying what properties something must have in order to fall under this concept. . . . The concept *square* is not a rectangle; only the objects which fall under this concept are rectangles; similarly the concept *black cloth* is neither black nor a cloth. Whether such objects exist is not immediately known by means of their definitions (GB, 125; also PMC, 90–91).

Heeding Frege's advice and imitating Quine's exercise on mention and use, I suggest the following two exercises designed to illustrate the differences between words, concepts, and objects. Capital letters are used in place of Frege's italics:

EXERCISE A: To mention the concept ROSE we use 'ROSE'. 'Rose' and 'ROSE' have four letters. 'A rose is a ROSE' is a statement containing 'rose' and 'ROSE' in which being a ROSE is predicated of a rose; ''A rose is a ROSE' is a ROSE'' is a false statement containing 'rose' and 'ROSE' in which being a ROSE is wrongly predicated of a statement. To mention a rose we use 'rose'. Although a rose by any other name would smell as sweet, neither that other name nor 'rose' would have a smell. Although this same rose that blooms today may tomorrow be dying, the concept ROSE is not time's fool and has seen countless such roses come and go.

To be compared with:

EXERCISE B: A lie, according to my dictionary, is a FALSE STATEMENT, something intended or serving to convey a false impression or a FLAT CONTRADICTION. 'A lie is a LIE' is a TRUE STATEMENT containing 'lie' and 'LIE'. ''A lie is a LIE' is a LIE'' is a FALSE STATEMENT because in it being a LIE is predicated of a true statement. The identity statement ''x' = 'y'' is a LIE according to the above dictionary definition. Though it courts paradox, 'x = y' may prove to be a TRUE STATEMENT when 'x' and 'y' name the same object.

CONCEPTS AND THE PRINCIPLE OF SUBSTITUTIVITY OF IDENTICALS

"I must first emphasize," Frege wrote, "the radical difference between concepts and objects, which is such that a concept can never stand for an object or an object for a concept" (PMC, 92).

"Objects and concepts are fundamentally different," he stated unequivocally, "and cannot stand in for one another. And the same goes for corresponding words or signs . . . concepts cannot stand in the same relations as objects. It would not be false, but impossible to think of them as doing so" (PW, 120). "The logical places for concepts are unsuitable for objects, and . . . the logical places for objects are unsuitable for concepts."[20]

Here Frege is making a direct reference to another important logical fact about concepts. Because concepts and objects are of different logical types, concepts could be reasonably expected to exhibit anomalous behavior when treated as objects. In particular, they might be expected to fail the substitutivity test. Identity "can only be thought of as holding for objects, not concepts" (PW, 120), Frege insisted. "We cannot properly speak of identity in the case of concepts" (PMC, 97).

One of the principal reasons why substitutivity fails, Frege argued, is that an identity statement is reversible. If $x = y$, then $y = x$. But the relation of an object's falling under a concept is an irreversible relation. It does not follow from the fact that x is a Y, that Y is a x (nor for that matter that y is an X). Using the expression 'the morning star' as a name, Frege used to the following example to make his point:

> In the sentence 'The morning star is Venus', we have two proper names, 'morning star' and 'Venus', for the same object. In the sentence 'the morning star is a planet' we have a proper name, 'the morning star,' and a concept-word, 'planet.' So far as language goes, no more has happened than that 'Venus' has been replaced by 'a planet'; but really the relation has become wholly different. An equation is reversible; an object's falling under a concept is an irreversible relation (GB, 44).

If the morning star is Venus, then Venus is the morning star. But though the morning star may be a PLANET, a planet is not necessarily the morning star. Aware of language's tendency to use concepts as objects, Frege appealed to another example to illustrate the differences:

> In the sentence 'there is at least one square root of 4,' we are saying something, not about (say) the definite number 2, nor about −2, but about a concept, *square root of 4*; viz. that it is not empty. . . . It need not then surprise us that the same sentence may be conceived as saying something about a concept and also as saying something about a object; only we must observe that *what* is being said is different. In the sentence 'there is at least one square root of 4' it is impossible to replace the words 'square root of 4' by 'the concept *square root of 4*'; i.e. what is suitably said of the concept does not suit the object. . . . Thus the words 'the concept *square root of 4*' have an essentially different behaviour, as regards possible substitution, from the words 'square root of 4' in our original sentence; i.e. the reference of the two phrases is essentially different (GB, 49–50).

Concepts are essentially predicative and it is their predicable nature that makes them refractory to principles of extensionality like the principle of substitutivity of identicals, and so constitutes their intensionality. Substitutivity presumes identity. There is no identity without entity. Given the particular role accorded to identity and substitutivity in logic since Frege, it is no wonder that people like Quine have asked what kind of objects intensions are an have been disturbed by their unobjectlike behavior.

The Evolution in Frege's Views on the
Differences Between Concepts and Objects

Frege, we have seen, emphasized "the radical difference between concepts and objects" (PMC, 92). One must "never lose sight of the distinction between concept and object," he warned in his 1884 *Foundations of Arithmetic;* "it is a mere illusion to suppose that a concept can be made into an object without altering it" (FA, x). He even devoted an entire article to spelling out the logical differences between concepts and objects in explicit terms (GB, 42-55). In particular, he stated unequivocally that "concepts cannot stand in the same relations as objects" (PW, 120), and he more than once insisted that "objects and concepts are fundamentally different and cannot stand in for one another" (PW, 120, 122; PMC, 92-93; GB, 50).

His repeated protests, however, thinly disguise his deeper struggle to come to terms with a specific difficulty involving concepts, objects, and identity, which he ran up against while working on the foundations of arithmetic. There was, he realized, "a great obstacle in the way of expressing ourselves correctly and making ourselves understood. If I want to speak of a concept, language with almost irresistible force compels me to use an inappropriate expression which obscures—I might almost say falsifies—the thought" (PW, 119). "By a kind of necessity of language . . . I mention an object when what I intend is a concept" (GB, 54, also 46). And he ultimately blamed this linguistic trap for the defeat of his logical project.

In spite of all his lucidity concerning logical differences between concepts and objects, this "idiosyncrasy of language" lured Frege to transform concepts into objects, and for a certain time he managed to convince himself that one really could "switch the roles of concept and object" (PW, 120), that although because of its predicative nature, a concept could not be an object, it could nonetheless "be converted into an object" or more precisely an object could "go proxy for it" (GB, 46).

Frege used identity statements to effect this transformation, reasoning that if one has two concepts Φ and Ψ, which fulfill the condition that if something is a Ψ then it is a Φ, and that if something is a Φ it is a Ψ, then such concepts can be correlated with objects in such a way that concepts that are mutually subordinate are correlated with the same object. He thought that this relation of mutual subordination had strong enough affinities with his idea of identity to compel "us almost ineluctably to transform a sentence in which mutual subordination is asserted of concepts into a sentence expressing an equality" (PW, 182).

Frege characterized the procedure he came to advocate in explicit terms writing in the early 1890s that:

> the relationship of equality, by which I understand complete coincidence, identity, can only be thought of as holding for objects, not concepts. If we say 'The meaning of the word "conic section" is the same as that of the concept-word "curve of the second degree" or 'The concept *conic section* coincides with the concept *curve of the second degree*', the words 'meaning of the concept-word "conic section"' are the name of an object, not of a concept; for their nature is not predicative, they are not unsaturated, they cannot be used with the indefinite article. The same goes for 'the concept *conic section*'. But although the relation of equality can only be thought of as holding for objects, there is an analogous relation for concepts. . . . We say that an object *a* is equal to an object *b* (in the sense of completely coinciding with it) if *a* falls under every concept under which *b* falls, and conversely. We obtain

something corresponding to this for concepts if we switch the roles of concept and object. We could then say that the relation we had in mind above holds between the concept ϕ and the concept X if every object that falls under ϕ also falls under X and conversely (PW, 120).

"In any sentence," he concluded, "we can substitute *salva veritate* one concept-word for another if they have the same extension, so that it is also the case in inference, and where the laws of logic are concerned, that concepts differ only in so far as their extensions are different. . . . Therefore just as proper names can replace one another *salva veritate,* so too can concept-words, if their extension is the same" (PW, 118). In granting this, Frege was conceding that what he deemed to be an irreversible relation, that of an object's falling under a concept, could be equivalent to the reversible relation of identity, that the logical places for objects could be suitable for concepts.

Frege, however, ultimately believed that this confusion of concept and object was the fatal flaw in his logical system. When asked shortly before his death to write on the paradoxes of set theory in order to provide further justification for his belief that it was untenable, Frege replied that "the essence of the procedure which leads to the thicket of contradictions" consisted in transforming a concept word into an object name or a proper name. He came to believe: "This is inadmissible because of the essential difference between concept and object, which is indeed quite covered up in our word languages. . . . Because of its need for completion, (unsaturatedness, predicative nature), a concept word is unsaturated, i.e., it contains a gap which is intended to receive a proper name. . . . Confusion is bound to arise if a concept word, as a result of its transformation into a proper name comes to be in a place for which it is unsuited" (PMC, 55). and:

> One feature of language that threatens to undermine the reliability of thinking is its tendency to form proper names to which no objects correspond. ... A particularly noteworthy example of this is the formation of a proper name after the pattern of 'the extension of the concept *star*'. Because of the definite article, this expression appears to designate an object; but there is no object for which this phrase could be a linguistically appropriate designation. ... The same expression—'the extension of the concept *star*'—serves at the same time to illustrate, in yet another way, the fatal tendency of language to form apparent proper names: 'the concept *star*' is, of itself, one such. The definite article creates the impression that this phrase is meant to designate an object, or, what amounts to the same thing, that 'the concept *star*' is a proper name, whereas 'concept *star*' is surely a designation of a concept and thus could not be more different from a proper name. The difficulties this idiosyncrasy of language entangles us in are incalculable (PW, 269–70).

Experience, Frege wrote in 1925, had shown him "how easily this can get one into a morass." He himself, he says, suffered this fate when he tried to place number theory on scientific foundations. When he had doubts, he confessed, he silenced them only to have the whole edifice collapse around him. "Such an event should be a warning not only to oneself but also to others," he concluded. "We must set up a warning sign visible from afar, let no one imagine that he can transform a concept into an object"

(PMC, 55, also PW, 269). However, ambiguities still lurking in the way the equals sign is used in canonical notation still make many aspects of Frege's plan seem more feasible than his experience proved them to be.

6

Equating Equality and Identity

According to dictionaries, two things are identical when they are the same in every way. They are equal when they are the same under a specific description, as given in a particular way. According to the dictionary definition, the difference between equality and identity would then be the difference between sharing any given property or properties, or having all properties in common. This is the ordinary, non-mathematical, use of the words 'equality' and 'identity'. For example, we commonly say that the United States of America was dedicated to the proposition that all men are created equal with respect to their legal rights, but I believe that no one has ever said, nor would be so foolish as to say, that all men are created identical.

Logicians, however, are not bound to observe common linguistic practice, and modern symbolic logic was created by mathematicians who remained closer to a mathematical understanding of equality. Frege set the course for most of those who followed after him by explicitly equating identity and equality (GB, 22–23, 56, 120–21, 141 n., 146 n., 159–61, 210; PMC, 141; FR, 327, 331; PW, 120–21, 182). In this chapter I examine certain difficulties that arise when identity is equated with lesser forms of equivalence in philosophical reasoning. In the next chapter I will study how Frege himself identified equality and identity in his philosophy of arithmetic.

Numerous examples can be found that illustrate the differences between equality and identity. One of the most obvious of these lies in the differences between a tautology and an informative identity statement. The informativeness of an identity statement having the form 'x = y' lies precisely in the fact that some difference, however small, is represented by the fact that two different symbols flank the equals sign. For such an identity statement to be both true and informative there must be something true represented by 'y' which was not represented by 'x'. Though only the thinnest of intensional margins may separate 'x' from 'y', the less trivial the difference represented by the use of the different symbols is, the more informative the statement will be.

So we are confronted with the following dilemma: the presence of two different signs for the same object in informative identity statements indicates that one of the signs is being used to tell us something of a given object that may not normally be indicated by using the other sign. This was surely part of what Frege meant when he wrote that "the many important applications of identity come from the fact that we can recognize as identical what is given to us in different ways" (FA, §67), and "different names for the same content are not always merely an indifferent matter of form; but rather if they are associated with different modes of determination, they touch the essence of the thing itself" (BS, §8).

Differences between equality and identity become much more tangible once we leave the realm of x's and y's, and a's and b's. There are, after all, few cases in which the difference between being called 'x' or being called 'y' really matters. However, the issues at stake become clearer when we consider the reference of the signs. Since identity statements are to be true or false only on the basis of what they stand for, this is surely something we are meant to do.

For instance, is a person in an irreversible coma following an accident who is entirely dependent on machines to sustain her bodily functions identical to the person she was before the accident took place? Think of the innumerable things that could be have been predicated of her before that are no longer true, and the truly macabre propositions that could result from substitution rules that do not take sufficient account of the difference between equality and identity. Her family surely would never have considered depriving her of the minimum means necessary to support her life before she was in the coma.

And, of course, differences between equality and identity do figure in many other dilemmas faced in medical practice today. Surely many of the most profound moral issues involved in abortion rights turn on whether a fetus is in all essential respects the same as the person that will develop from it if the pregnancy is not terminated. Such contexts make it hard to dismiss differences between equality and identity as being merely linguistic or psychological.

LOGICAL ABSTRACTION, CLASSES, AND EXTENSIONALITY

Logical maneuvers by which a lesser form of equivalence becomes equated with identity have played a fundamental role in logic since Frege began writing such devices into the foundations for logic, mathematics, and philosophy in his *Foundations of Arithmetic* (§§62–69). One such technique that has proved particularly attractive is logical abstraction,[21] a procedure whereby, as Quine explains, given a condition '——' upon x, we form the class $\hat{x}$—whose members are just those objects x which satisfy the condition. The operator '$\hat{x}$' may be read 'the class of all objects x such that'. The class $\hat{x}$—— is definable, by description, as *the* class y to which any object x will belong if and only if —— (FLPV, 87).

In logical abstraction a property is singled out, and the particular equivalence obtaining between objects possessing this property comes to be regarded as an identity (on paper). A common predicate is interpreted as a common relation to a new term, the class of all those terms that are equal in terms of the property indicated by the predicate. The class of terms having the given relation then replaces the common property inferred from the equivalence relation chosen, and all the other properties that might have normally served to distinguish those objects from each other, or from other objects equal to them in the same respect, are "abstracted" out of the picture. Once deleted on paper, the properties that originally might have marked any difference between the mere equality and the full identity of x and y are presumably expected to simplify matters by vanishing entirely from the reasoning.

Quine has provided this example of how the procedure might be applied in actual practice:

> It may happen that a theory dealing with nothing but concrete individuals can conveniently be reconstrued as treating of universals, by the method of identifying indiscernibles. Thus consider a theory of bodies compared in point of length. The values of the bound variables are physical objects, and the only predicate is 'L', where 'Lxy' means 'x is longer than y'. Now where $\sim Lxy \cdot \sim Lyx$, anything that can

be truly said of x within this theory holds equally for y and vice versa. Hence it is convenient to treat '$\sim\!Lxy \cdot \sim\!Lyx$' as '$x = y$'. Such identification amounts to reconstruing the values of our variables as universals, namely lengths, instead of physical objects (FLPV, 117).

The talk of universals engaged in, Quine explains, may be regarded "merely as a manner of speaking—through the metaphorical use of the identity sign for what is really not identity but sameness of length. . . . In abstracting universals by identification of indiscernibles, we do no more than rephrase the same old system of particulars" (FLPV, 118).

Many have found abstraction to be a convenient way of translating various familiar expressions, and those having to do with numbers especially, into the notation of the extensional logic favored by so many logicians. Through it, one might introduce new objects into reasoning by translating many expressions into extensional language that would not on the surface seem to lend themselves to extensional treatment. Talk of properties is transformed into talk of classes as every monadic predicate comes to have a class as an extension—the class of all things of which the predicate is true. The notation Fy comes to mean y is a member of the class F, the class of all objects fulfilling a given condition—the class of those things that are equal in that particular respect (FLPV, 120–21). Many things people want to accomplish can, in fact, be accomplished by leaving unwanted properties out of the picture (and, one might add, might not be accomplishable were they properly taken into account).

However convenient a device abstraction may appear to be, though, abstracting away the differences between equality and identity creates some very fundamental problems of its own. For instance, as Quine writes of the process described in the text just cited: "[T]his innocent kind of abstraction is inadequate to abstracting any but mutually exclusive classes. For when a class is abstracted by this method what holds it together is the indistinguishability of its members by the terms of the theory in question; so any overlapping of two such classes would fuse them irretrievably into a single class" (FLPV, 118). This outcome is hardly surprising when one considers that the abstraction process robs objects of all their individuality. The members of the class formed by abstraction are identical, indiscernible, and interchangeable precisely because they have been logically stripped of whatever might distinguish them, the criteria by which any difference between them might be discerned having been disposed of.

Left unadulterated, definitions by abstraction also suffer from ambiguity due to the radical amount of information lost when the abstraction was effected. For one thing, in suppressing properties, abstraction has suppressed information needed to secure a reference for the terms in many, if not most, contexts. We no longer have enough information about our object to identify it uniquely, or to identify it as the same again when characterized in even a slightly different way. For one might fairly ask where all those officious properties that marked the differences between equality and identity actually went, and what the consequences might be if they did not just cease to be because they were in the way. What is there to keep banished properties from slipping back into the picture to cause basic principles of inference like substitutivity and existential generalization to fail?

So tight control over abstraction is called for in the form of extensional principles ensuring that the new objects formed will behave as if they were the same in every way. Since what is needed for substitution is that everything that can be said of the reference of 'x' can be said of the reference of 'y', what is wanted is a principle of extensionality stipulating that classes are identical when their members are identical, that any two predicates that agree extensionally, i.e., are true of the same objects, will be interchangeable salva veritate. Such a rule promises to make the principles of substitutivity of identicals and existential generalization vital to extensional logic operative. Predicate letters would acquire the privileges of ordinary variables. The truth value of sentences formed from simple predicates and relational expressions would come to depend only on the truth value of their component parts.

However, although such a rule may keep failures of substitutivity from occurring, it may well itself give rise to new perplexities since the condition for membership in the class to begin with was only that the objects be equal in a given respect, and not really identical at all. Although it may be plain that some identity is involved when the class of featherless bipeds is said to be the same as the class of men, the presence of "some identity" is part of the definition of equality, and does not in and of itself suffice to make the members of those classes identical. It was only a logical sleight of the hand that declared them identical in the first place.

Quine points out another problem with abstraction in this passage from *Mathematical Logic* where he explains how easily class abstraction leads to Russell's paradox:

> The usual way of specifying a class is by citing a necessary and sufficient condition for membership in it. Such is the method when one speaks of "the class of all entities x such that . . . ," appending one or another matrix. The class of all entities x such that x writes poems, e.g., is the class of poets. . . . Despite its sanction from the side of usage and common sense, however, this method of specifying classes leads to trouble. Applied to certain matrices, the

prefix 'the class of all entities x such that' produces expressions which cannot consistently be regarded as designating any class whatever. One matrix of this kind, discovered by Russell, is '$\sim(x \in x)$'; there is no such thing as the class of all entities x such that $\sim(x \in x)$. For suppose w were such a class. For every entity x, then,

$$x \in w. = \sim(x \in x)$$

Taking x in particular as w itself, we are led to the contradiction:

$$w \in w. = \sim(w \in w).^{22}$$

Marcus on Distinguishing between Identity and Weaker Forms of Equivalence

Ruth Barcan Marcus[23] has been one of the staunchest and most eloquent advocates of lucidity regarding the differences between identity and weaker forms of equivalence that explicit or implicit extensionalizing principles would extinguish. As part of her ongoing campaign to expand classical logic to deal with larger areas of discourse, she has drawn attention to ambiguities regarding equality and identity that have slipped into logical reasoning and are present there now. In particular, she has drawn attention to the extent to which extensional logical systems are dependent on (1) directly or indirectly imposing restrictions prohibiting some intensional functions, and (2) equating identity with a weaker form of equivalence.

"The usual reason given for reducing identity to equality," she writes, "is that it provides a simpler base for mathematics, mathematics being concerned with aggregates discussed in truth functional contexts, not with predicates in intensional contexts. Under such restrictive conditions, the substitution theorem can generally be proved for equal (formally equivalent) classes, with the result that equality functions *as* identity. Establishing the foundations of mathematics is not the only purpose of logic, particularly if the assumptions deemed convenient for mathematics do violence to both ordinary and philosophical usage."[24]

Extensionality, Marcus explains, has acquired the undeserved reputation of being a clear, unambiguous concept, and as such well-suited to the needs of mathematics and the empirical sciences where, it is claimed, there is no need to traffic in fuzzy, troublesome non-extensional notions. However, she points out, no single well-defined theory of extensionality exists but only stronger and weaker principles of extensionality. And she urges "that the distinctions between stronger and weaker equivalences be made explicit before, for one avowed reason or another, they are obliterated",[25] a request that would seem to be in keeping with the requirements of a logic that prides itself on its clarity and was devised to keep ambiguity from creeping unawares into reasoning.

Drawing attention to some undesirable consequences of failing to distinguish between identity and lesser forms of equivalence in the medical sciences is one way of illustrating Marcus's concerns and of demonstrating the real need for consciously trafficking in intensional notions in order to control confusion and draw the fine distinctions that are both germane and indispensable to many scientific undertakings. Strong extensional principles may prove appropriate in certain contexts, e.g., in criminal investigations or judicial proceedings where a person's guilt or innocence may be the sole determinant factor, but relying on them could have disastrous consequences in other contexts. For instance, in medical research and practice, extensional notions could unnecessarily complicate situations and generate confusion and even make the difference between life and death, sickness and health.

Consider this example. Doctors at Toronto's Hospital for Sick Children have discovered that the immune system of certain diabetics identifies a protein present on the surface of their insulin-producing cells as being the same as a protein present in cow's milk with which it is in many respects almost identical. Unable to distinguish between the two proteins, the immune system stimulates the body to attack and destroy its own insulin-producing cells in the pancreas, causing juvenile onset diabetes, which may lead to blindness, kidney failure, and heart disease.

Here Marcus's arguments are most apropos, for the immune systems in question are identifying two proteins as being the same on the basis of compelling similarities; they are not picking out essential differences between the milk protein and the protein on the insulin-producing cells. In a case like this, equating identity with lesser forms of equivalence is having disastrous consequences for diabetics.

Intensional factors marking the differences between identity and lesser forms of equivalence also come into play in organ transplant operations where what is sought are organs that are alike in certain respects but surely not identical to the diseased or defective organs they are meant to replace. A strong enough equivalence may obtain between different organs of the same type so that the host organism will not reject the transplanted organ as foreign because it is sufficiently like the organ it supplants. It is precisely intensional considerations that mark the difference between unwanted strict identity and the sought-after equivalence powerful enough to keep substitutivity of the organs from breaking down. To say of organ x that it has all the properties in common with organ y essential for a successful transplant is to make a weaker claim than to claim they are identical.

There is a real need to traffic in non-extensional notions to achieve clarity regarding major philosophical issues in many fields. For attempts to disregard the differences between equality and identity do not work in ways that have yet to be fully mapped out. It is plain to see that in the above two cases doctors and medical researchers could not seriously consider resorting to any conceptual tool that was so blunt, crude, and blind as to systematically disregard the differences between identity and lesser forms of equivalence. Anyone insisting on deintensionalizing the medical situations just cited would surely inspire contempt in the scientific community, which, fortunately, would not rely on so crude a conceptual instrument in situations that cry out for the conscious intensional adjustment and progressive refinement of a conceptual tool that less finely tuned could have disastrous consequences. The blithe use of extensional notions could, in the case of the organ transplant operation, be dangerous enough to cause a patient to die of post-operative complications due to simplistic ideas about extensionality and scientific thinking.

Deintensionalizing logic by suppressing the properties marking the difference between full identity and mere equality means suppressing information that may be not only germane but vital to much philosophical reasoning. However inconvenient they may be on paper, and however uncongenial they may be to some philosophers, intensions can be the decisive factor in real life situations where failure to resort to them is sure to increase perplexity, engender confusion, and complicate matters instead of bringing clarity and precision. One of the main purposes of the next part of this book is to more explicitly connect attempts to shun intensions and shove reasoning into a strongly extensional mold with the questions raised by both the paradoxes that led Frege to abandon his logical foundations for arithmetic and paradoxes associated with modality and intensionality.

II

The Quest for a Clear Extensional Ontology

7

Identity and Frege's
Foundations for Arithmetic

Arithmetic, Frege told his readers in his preface to the *Begriffs-schrift*, had been the point of departure for his work to develop a symbolic language whose first purpose it would be "to provide us with the most reliable test of the validity of a chain of inference and to point out every proposition that tries to sneak in unnoticed, so that its origin might be investigated." "That is why," he wrote of the new symbolic language unveiled in his book, "I intend to apply it first of all to that science to provide a more detailed analysis of the concepts of arithmetic and a deeper foundation for its theorems."[26]

As Frege's work to accomplish his goal progressed, identity came to play an increasingly important role in his thought in a way that raised certain challenging questions. And he finally capitalized on ambiguities inherent in identity statements to make his ideas work.

Identity considerations also would figure prominently among the reasons Frege eventually gave for abandoning his life's work. In this chapter I take a close look at the role identity played in Frege's theory of arithmetic and the reasons he ultimately gave for abandoning his theories.

IDENTITY AND SUBSTITUTIVITY IN
FREGE'S THEORY OF ARITHMETIC

"With numbers," Frege explained as he began outlining his theory of arithmetic in the *Foundations of Arithmetic*, "it is a matter of fixing the sense of an identity" (FA, x; §§62, 106). Numbers, he begins his argument, are independent objects (FA, §55) that figure as such in identity statements like '$1 + 1 = 2$'. Although in everyday discourse numbers are often used as adjectives rather than as nouns, in arithmetic, he affirms, their independent status is apparent at every turn, and any appearance to the contrary "can always be got around." For instance, he contended, the statement 'Jupiter has four moons' can be rewritten as 'the number of Jupiter's moons is four'. In this new version the word 'is' is not the copula, but the 'is' of identity and means 'is identical with' or 'is the same as'. "So," he maintained, "what we have is an identity, stating that the expression 'the number of Jupiter's moons' signifies the same object as the word 'four'." Using the same reasoning he concluded that Columbus is identical with the discoverer of America for "it is the same man that we call Columbus and the discoverer of America" (FA, §57). For Frege, remember, names and descriptions are of the same type level and can be meaningfully equated.

Once Frege was satisfied that he had established numbers as independent objects and acquired a set of meaningful statements in which a number is recognized as being the same again, he turned to the question of establishing a criterion for deciding in all cases whether b was the same as a. For him this meant defining the sense of the statement: "the number which belongs to the concept F is the same as that which belongs to the concept G." This, he believed, would provide a general criterion for the identity of numbers (FA, §62).

Not wanting to introduce a special definition of identity for this, but wishing rather "to use the concept of identity, taken as already known, as a means for arriving at that which is to be regarded as being identical" (FA, §63), Frege explicitly adopted Leibniz's principle that "things are the same as each other, of which one can be substituted for the other without loss of truth" (FA, §65). Of his choice he wrote:

> This I propose to adopt as my own definition of equality. Whether we use 'the same', as Leibniz does, or 'equal', is not of any importance. 'The same', may indeed be thought to refer to complete agreement in all respects, 'equal', only to agreement in this respect or that; but we can adopt a form of expression such that this distinction vanishes. For example, instead of 'the segments are equal in length', we can say 'the length of the segments is equal', or 'the same', and instead of 'the surfaces are equal in color', 'the color of the surfaces is equal'. . . . [I]n universal substitutability all the laws of identity are contained (FA, §65).[27]

So even as Frege was writing Leibniz's formula right into the foundations of his logic, he modified Leibniz's dictum in an important way that, as I hope to show, has presented thorny problems for those who have tried to further Frege's insights and answer some of the really hard questions his logic raises. For although Leibniz's law defines identity—a complete coincidence—Frege, here as elsewhere, explicitly maintains that for him "whether we use 'the same' as Leibniz does, or 'equal' is not of any importance. 'The same' may indeed be thought to refer to complete agreement in all respects, 'equal' only to agreement in this respect or that" (FA, §65).

Not one to adhere slavishly to usual linguistic practice, Frege departed from ordinary usage insisting over and over that for him there was no difference between equality and identity (GB, 22–23, 56, 120–21, 141 n., 146 n., 159–61, 210; PMC, 141; PW, 120–21, 182). In the preface to his 1893 *Basic Laws of Arithmetic* (p. ix), he explains that he has chosen to use the ordinary sign of equality in his symbolic language because he has convinced himself that it is used in arithmetic to mean the very thing that he wished to symbolize. "In fact," he wrote there, "I use the expression 'equal' to mean the same as 'coinciding or identical with' and this is just how the sign of equality is actually used in arithmetic."

Moreover, Frege dismissed any possible objections to this procedure as resting on an inadequate distinction between sign and signified. "It is true," he explained, "that in the equation $2^2 = 2 + 2$ the sign on the left is different from the one on the right, but both signs designate or refer to the same number" (BL, ix; GB, 121, also GB, 22). (In a note to this statement Frege significantly adds that he also says that the two signs differ in sense but that the meaning or reference is the same).

Frege believed that by rewriting the sentences of ordinary language, the differences between equality and identity could be made to vanish. So in the passage cited above he has recommended rewriting the sentence 'The segments are equal in length' as 'the length of the segments is equal or the same', and 'the surfaces are identical in color' as 'the color of the surfaces is identical'.

Since Frege further maintained it to be "actually the case that in universal substitutability all the laws of identity were contained" (FA, §65), to justify his definition he believed he only needed "to show that it is possible, if line a is parallel to line b, to substitute 'the direction of line b' everywhere for 'the direction of line a'. This task is made simpler," he conceded, "by the fact that we are being taken initially to know of nothing that can be asserted about the direction of a line except the one thing, that it coincides with the direction of some other line. We should thus have to show only that substitution was possible in an identity of this one type, or in judgement-contents containing such identities as constituent elements" (FA, §65).

In these examples Frege transforms statements about objects that are equal under a certain description into statements expressing complete identity. By erasing the difference between identity and equality he is in fact arguing that being the same in any one way is equivalent to being the same in all ways. However, he realized that many of the inferences that could be made by appealing to such a principle would lead to evidently false and absurd conclusions.

THE PROBLEMS FREGE ADDRESSED
FROM THE BEGINNING

Frege himself acknowledged that left unmodified the procedure just described was liable to produce nonsensical conclusions or be sterile and unproductive (FA §66-67). For example, he realized that his definition of identity only afforded logicians a means of recognizing an object as the same again if determined in a different way, but it did not account for all the ways in which it could be determined. To illustrate some nonsensical consequences of defining identity in this way, he carries the reasoning involved in his example of the identity of two lines one step further. However, the points he wishes to make can be made more graphically by leaving the world of abstract geometrical figures for denizens of a more material one.

So, parroting Frege's reasoning in *Foundations of Arithmetic* §66, I propose to illustrate his point about possible nonsensical consequences of his definition by appealing to a more concrete case. Suppose it has finally been determined to be true that:

'the man who fired the shots from behind the grassy knoll is identical with the man who killed John Kennedy'

Frege's definition of identity would then afford us a means of identifying the man who fired the shots from behind the grassy knoll again in those cases in which he is referred to as the man who killed John Kennedy. But, as Frege recognized, this means does not provide for all the cases. For instance it could not decide for us whether Lee Harvey Oswald was the man who fired the shots from behind the grassy knoll. While any informed person would consider it perfectly nonsensical to confuse Lee Harvey Oswald with the man who fired the shots from behind grassy knoll, this would not, Frege would acknowledge, be owing to his definition. For it says nothing as to whether the statement

'the man who fired the shots from behind the grassy knoll is identical with Lee Harvey Oswald'

should be affirmed or denied, except for the one case where Lee Harvey Oswald is given in the form of 'the man who killed John Kennedy'. Only if we could lay it down that if Lee Harvey Oswald was not the man who killed John Kennedy (still following Frege's reasoning), could our statement be denied, while if he was that man, our original definition would decide whether it is to be affirmed or denied. But then we have obviously come around in a circle, Frege acknowledged. For in order to make use of this definition we should have to know already in every case whether the statement 'Lee Harvey Oswald is identical with the man who killed John Kennedy' was to be affirmed or denied.

Left as it was his definition was unproductive, Frege further judged, because in adopting this way out, we would be presupposing that an object can only be given in one single way. For otherwise, (still parroting Frege's reasoning, but using our more material example) it would not follow, from the fact that Lee Harvey Oswald was not introduced by our definition that he could not have been by means of it. "All identities would then amount simply to this," Frege then wrote, "that whatever is given to us in the same way is to be reckoned as the same. This is, however, a principle so obvious and sterile as not to be worth stating. We could not, in fact, draw from it any conclusion which was not the same as one of our premises." Surely though, he concluded, identities play such an important role in so many fields "because we are able to recognize something as the same again even although it is given in a different way" (FA, §§67, 107).

So seeing that he could not by these methods alone obtain concepts with sharp limits to their application, nor therefore, for the same reasons, any satisfactory concept of number either, Frege felt obliged to introduce extensions to guarantee that an identity holding between two concepts could be transformed into an identity of extensions and conversely (FA, §§67, 107).

However, Frege wrote of extensions at the end of the *Foundations of Arithmetic:* "This way of getting over the difficulty cannot be expected to meet universal approval, and many will prefer other methods of removing the doubt in question. I attach no decisive importance even to bringing in the extensions of concepts at all" (FA, §107).

ON FREGE'S WAY OUT

Although Frege ended the *Foundations of Arithmetic* claiming that he was not attaching any decisive importance to bringing in extensions, by the time it came to actually proving his theory of number in the *Basic Laws of Arithmetic* (BL, 5, 7, 129, §§38–47), extensions had taken on "great fundamental importance." Their introduction, he now maintained was "an important advance which makes for far greater flexibility" (BL, ix-x). "In fact," he wrote there, "I even define number itself as the extension of a concept, and extensions of concepts are, according to my definitions, graphs. So we just cannot do without graphs" (BL, x).

In *Basic Laws*, he argued that the generality of an identity could always be transformed into an identity of courses-of-values and conversely, an identity of courses-of-values may always be transformed into the generality of an identity. By this he meant that if it is true that $(x) F(x) = G(x)$, then those two functions have the same extension and that functions having the same extension are identical (BL, §§9, 21). "This possibility," he wrote, "must be regarded as a law of logic, a law that is invariably employed, even if tacitly, whenever discourse is carried on about extension of concepts. The whole Leibniz-Boole calculus of logic rests upon it. One might perhaps regard this transformation as unimportant or even as dispensable. As against this, I recall the fact that in my *Grundlagen der Arithmetik* I defined a Number as the extension of a concept. . . ." (BL, §9).

In an article on the logical paradoxes of set theory he was working on in 1906, Frege characterizes his theory of extensionality writing:

> Let the letters 'Φ' and 'Ψ' stand in for concept-words (*nomina appellativa*). Then we designate subordination in sentences of the form 'If something is Φ, then it is a Ψ'. In sentences of the form 'If something is a Φ, then it is a Ψ and if something is a Ψ then it is a Φ we designate mutual subordination, a second level relation, which has strong affinities with the first level relation of equality (identity). . . . And this compels us almost ineluctably to transform a sentence in which mutual subordination is asserted of concepts into a sentence expressing an equality.
>
> Admittedly, to construe mutual subordination simply as equality is forbidden. . . . Only in the case of objects can there be any question of equality (identity). And so the said transformation can only occur by concepts being correlated with objects in such a way that concepts which are mutually sub-

ordinate are correlated with the same object (PW, 181–82).

In §§146–47 of the 1903 *Basic Laws II* he characterized extensionality writing: "If a (first-level) function (of one argument) and another function are such as always to have the same value for the same argument, then we may say instead that the graph of the first is the same as that of the second. We are then recognizing something common to the two functions. . . . We must regard it as a fundamental law of logic that we are justified in thus recognizing something common to both, and that accordingly we may transform an equality holding generally into an equation (identity)" (GB, 159–60).

Frege never believed that any proof could be supplied that would sanction such a transformation. So he devised Basic Law V to mandate the view of identity, equality and substitutivity his system required. By transforming "a sentence in which mutual subordination is asserted of concepts into a sentence expressing an equality," Basic Law V would permit logicians to pass from a concept to its extension, a transformation which, Frege held, could "only occur by concepts being correlated with objects in such a way that concepts which are mutually subordinate are correlated with the same object" (PW, 182).

Frege gave as an example the sentence: 'Every square root of 1 is a binomial coefficient of the exponent –1 and every binomial coefficient of the exponent –1 is a square root of 1'. According to his theory this sentence is to be rewritten as 'The extension of the concept *square root of 1* is equal to (coincides with) the extension of the concept *binomial coefficient of the exponent –1*'. The words 'the extension of the concept *square root of 1*' are now to be regarded as a proper name as, Frege claimed, is indicated by the definite article. Such a transformation, he wrote, acknowledges that there is one and only one object designated by the proper name. Frege goes on to explain: "By permitting the transformation, you concede that such proper names have meanings. But by what right does such a transformation take place, in which concepts correspond to extensions of concepts, mutual subordination to equality. An actual proof can scarcely be furnished. We will have to assume an unprovable law here. Of course it isn't as self-evident as one would wish for a law of logic. And if it was possible for there to be doubts previously, these doubts have been reinforced by the shock the law has sustained from Russell's paradox" (PW, 182).

Strong Extensionality

Now that we have looked at Frege's characterization of extensionality, it is important to look at how extensions could help Frege solve the particular problems with identity and substitutivity in connection with which they were introduced in the *Foundations of Arithmetic*.

First of all, Frege was conscious of the fact that the logician's job was initially made simpler because she initially only had to recognize the object as given in the particular way stipulated by her identity statement. But Frege realized that his definition afforded no means of recognizing that object as the same again when given in a different way. So returning to our Kennedy example, suppose that the wife of a man who fired at Kennedy from behind the grassy knoll has come forward with incontrovertible evidence that her husband, one Mr. Knoll, fired shots at Kennedy and killed him. She was actually with her husband behind the grassy knoll that day but was too blinded by love for him to tell the police what she knew. She also wanted to protect her family. But Mr. Knoll has since died and her conscience is tormenting her. In addition to her eyewitness account she has produced authentic diaries in which her husband gave details of his plans. So, (changing the descriptions to expressions that name directly so as to avoid any problems deriving solely from the fact that descriptions appear in the putative identity statement)

'Mr. Knoll is identical with Kennedy's assassin'

is a true statement. Initially, it looks as if the case is closed. We can now substitute Mr. Knoll's name every time we find a reference to Kennedy's assassin. However, our identity statement is completely blind as concerns other alternatives. And once we give the matter further thought we find that Kennedy's assassin has so often been identified with Lee Harvey Oswald that substitution in most contexts would yield nonsense. For example, most of the Warren Report would become complete nonsense.

Now let us look at Frege's second point regarding the sterility of the procedure. It is certain that the single fact given by our identity is a highly informative statement. But just because our x is both F and G, this does not mean that if something is F it is G. We have learned only that Mr. Knoll killed Kennedy. But only on paper has Basic Law V ruled out the possibility that Lee Harvey Oswald, or someone else, might also have fired at Kennedy, and so might also have been Kennedy's assassin. Kennedy did not die instantly, and numerous factors may have finally conspired to bring about his death.

With Frege's principle of extensionality, however, we put on logical blinders. It mandates that since Mr. Knoll is identical to Kennedy's assassin, then any one who was Kennedy's assassin was Mr. Knoll. Our concepts have acquired the sharp limits our quest for knowledge and substitution requires (FA, §67; also §107). Which is all fine on paper, but extensionality will not of itself keep Lee Harvey Oswald from slipping back into the picture as, for example, someone who might also have been Kennedy's assassin, but was definitely not Mr. Knoll. It may seem at first attractively simple to obliterate distinctions between identity and equality, but the differences between x and y when they are joined together by the equals sign to make an informative statement do not just go away because we have a rule stipulating that equality is to function as identity. For informative identity statements are the breeding ground of contradictions in extensional systems. The seed of contradictions derivable in extensional systems lies buried in them—something, of course, wholly unacceptable to Frege, a man who developed a symbolic language whose stated first purpose was to provide "the most reliable test of validity for a chain of inferences and to point out every presupposition that tries to sneak in unnoticed" (BS, 6).

THE SHAKING OF FREGE'S
FOUNDATIONS FOR ARITHMETIC

Knowing the central role Frege accorded to fixing the sense of an identity and of the link he made between substitutivity and identity in his theory of arithmetic, and knowing that Frege ultimately concluded that there were irremediable flaws in the foundations for arithmetic he had proposed, it is important to look at the connections between Frege's views on identity and the reasons he gave for his despair regarding the tenability of his logical theories. The philosophical questions involving identity here are surely in this way tied into fundamental matters of vital concern to many philosophers in this century. Next I explore what Frege himself came to believe was the fatal flaw in his reasoning.

When Russell informed him of the famous paradox of set theory (PMC, 130–31), Frege immediately traced the origin of the contradiction to his axiom of extensionality, Basic Law V. In a letter written just six days after Russell's letter, Frege replied to Russell that the contradiction indicated "that the transformation of an identity into an identity of ranges of values (sect. 9 of my *Basic Laws*) is not always permissible, that my law V (sect. 20, p. 36) is false. . . . The collapse of my law V seems to undermine not only the foundations of my arithmetic but the only possible foundation of arithmetic as such. And yet, I should think it must be possible to set up conditions for the transformation of the generality of an identity into an identity of ranges of values so as to retain the essential of my proofs" (PMC, 132).

Frege initially expressed his conviction that a solution to the problems raised by Russell's paradox might be found (BL, 132; PMC, 73, 132), and he finally proposed one that involved a modification of the problematic law (BL, 139–43; GB, 214–24).

Frege had never been completely satisfied with Basic Law V, and he more than once admitted that he had formulated it because he saw no other way of logically grounding arithmetic other than by appealing to the extensions of concepts he had reticently began using in §68 of his *Foundations of Arithmetic* (FA, §105). When he published the first volume of the *Basic Laws of Arithmetic* in 1893, he was more explicit about his reservations: "If anyone should find anything defective," he wrote there, "he must be able to state precisely where, according to him, the error lies. . . . A dispute can arise, so far as I can see, only with regard to my Basic Law concerning courses of values (V)." This is where, he believed, the decision would be ultimately made (BL, vii; GB, 118). In his 1903 appendix to the second volume of the *Basic Laws of Arithmetic,* he wrote that he had never disguised from himself that it lacked the self-evidence that belonged to his other axioms and that he would have dispensed with it if he had known of any substitute for it (BL, 127; GB, 214).

Frege also set out to track down precisely what it was about Basic Law V that leads to the paradoxes (GB, 217). In the several texts in which he pinpoints what he believed was the source of the difficulties, he consistently cites Basic Law V's transformation of concepts into objects for extensional treatment as being at fault (PMC, 54–56, 191; PW, 181–82, 269–70). The discovery of the paradox indicated to Frege that Basic Law V was false, he recounted in the appendix to *Basic Laws of Arithmetic II* (GB, 214–24). The way he had introduced extensions was not legitimate (GB, 219), and the interpretation he had so far put on the words 'extension of a concept' needed to be corrected.

He searched for the origin of the contradiction (GB, 217). There was nothing, he decided, to stop him from transforming an equality holding between two concepts into an equality of extensions in conformity with the first part of his law, but from the fact that concepts are equal in extension, we cannot infer that whatever falls under one falls under the other. The extension may fall under only one of the two concepts whose extension it is. This can in no way be avoided, and so the second part of his law fails (GB, 214 n.f, 218–23). "If in general, for any first-level concept, we may speak of its extension, then the case arises of concepts having the same extension, although not all objects that fall under one fall under the other as well. This, however, really abolishes the extension of the concept," he concluded (GB, 221).

To illustrate Frege's point more clearly, we might turn to the modern analogue of his 'the number of Jupiter's moons is 4', i.e., the putative identity statement Quine made famous:

(1) '9 is the number of the planets'.

According to Basic Law V, supposing this to be a true identity, the number that belongs to the concept 9 is the same as that which belongs to the concept the number of the planets. But the converse does not necessarily hold. For though 9 may be the number of the planets, we cannot infer that whatever falls under one falls under the other. There is nothing other than Basic Law V to guarantee that all objects that fall under '9' fall under 'the number of the planets' as well. For instance, according to materialistic astronomy:

(2) The ninth planet, Pluto, was discovered in 1930.
(3) The planet Pluto may be an anomaly and not a planet at all, but a giant asteroid flung into its present position when it had a close gravitational encounter with one of the outer planets.
(4) A Planet X may exist far beyond Pluto, which would explain apparent irregularities in Neptune's orbit.
(5) According to astronomers the dark matter accounting for more than 90% of the total mass of the universe could be made of giant planets.

So, while Frege's Basic Law V would secure for us that all objects that fall under '9' fall under 'the number of the planets' as well, according to materialistic astronomy, by substitution into (1) 9 may equal 8, or 10, or an as yet undetermined number of planets. And this indeterminacy causes Frege's system to go haywire.

Frege finally decided that all efforts to repair his logical edifice were destined to failure (PW, 176). In 1912, having already given up trying to save his logic, he wrote for an article by Philip Jourdain:

> And now we know that when classes are introduced, a difficulty, (Russell's contradiction) arises. . . . Only with difficulty did I resolve to introduce classes (or extents of concepts) because the matter did not appear to me to be quite secure — and rightly so as it turned out. The laws of numbers are to be developed in a purely logical manner. But numbers are objects. . . . Our first aim was to obtain objects out of concepts, namely extents of concepts

or classes. By this I was constrained to overcome my resistance and to admit the passage from concepts to their extents. . . . I confess . . . I fell into the error of letting go too easily my initial doubts (PMC, 191).

Frege was convinced that "everybody who in his proofs has made use of extensions of concepts, classes, sets," was in the same position he was (GB, 214). He never believed that his law about extensions recovered from the shock it had received from Russell's paradox (PW, 182). Shortly before his death, Frege wrote in a letter: "The expressions 'the extension of F' seems naturalized by reason of its manifold employment and certified by science . . . but experience has shown how easily this can get one into a morass. I am among those who have suffered this fate. When I tried to place number theory on scientific foundations, I found such an expression very convenient. While I sometimes had slight doubts during the execution of the work, I paid no attention to them. And so it happened that after the completion of the *Basic Laws of Arithmetic* the whole edifice collapsed around me" (PMC, 55).

8

Russell on the Origins of the Set-theoretical Paradoxes

Intellectual sorrow descended upon Bertrand Russell in full measure early in 1901. The cause: a contradiction about classes that are not members of themselves which had managed to slip into Frege's foundations for arithmetic.[28] A year later, Russell wrote of his finding to Frege, who immediately wrote back to him that the discovery had surprised him beyond words and left him thunderstruck because it rocked the very ground on which he had hoped to build arithmetic (PMC, 130-32).

Russell's discovery eventually led Frege to give up all his efforts to provide secure logical foundations for arithmetic and to conclude that his endeavors had been a complete failure (PMC, 176). The discovery also had a dramatic effect on the work being done by other mathematicians. David Hilbert, who had been prepared for the discovery in advance by Georg Cantor,[29] and whose colleague Ernst Zermelo had independently uncovered the contradiction at about the same time Russell had,[30] has provided a vivid firsthand account of the reaction to the Zermelo's and Russell's finding:

> In their joy over the new and rich results, mathematicians apparently had not examined critically enough whether the modes of inference employed were admissible; for purely through the ways in which notions were formed and modes of inference used—ways that in time had become customary—

contradictions appeared, sporadically at first, then ever more severely and ominously. They were the paradoxes of set theory, as they are called. In particular, a contradiction discovered by Zermelo and Russell had, when it became known, a downright catastrophic effect in the world of mathematics. Confronted with these paradoxes, Dedekind and Frege actually abandoned their standpoint and quit the field; for a long time Dedekind had reservations about permitting a new edition of his epoch-making booklet, and Frege, too, was forced to recognize that the tendency of his book was mistaken, as he confesses in an appendix. . . . The reaction was so violent that the commonest and most fruitful notions and the very simplest and most important modes of inference in mathematics were threatened and their use was to be prohibited. . . . Just think: in mathematics, this paragon of reliability and truth, the very notions and inferences, as everyone learns, teaches and uses them, lead to absurdities. And where else would reliability and truth be found if even mathematical thinking fails?[31]

Russell himself concluded that the solution of the contradictions seemed to be possible only "by adopting theories which might be true but were not beautiful," and that once the contradictions were discovered the "splendid certainty" that he had always hoped to find in mathematics had become lost in a "bewildering maze."[32]

Paradoxes analogous to the ones Russell, Zermelo, and others discovered as being derivable within set theory can easily be fashioned out of natural languages and have been known since antiquity.[33] But the fact that such a basic antinomy of the kind they and others were finding could be derived within the rigorous, exacting theories being developed at the time was sufficiently disturbing to suggest to mathematicians that there were deep underlying problems that needed to be found and could not be ignored.

In earlier chapters, I examined Frege's ideas as to the problems in his logic which have led to puzzles, antinomies, contradictions, and paradoxes that have exercised philosophers ever since his theories were submitted to close scrutiny. In the next two chapters, I follow Russell in his efforts to track down the errors he believed Frege had allowed to creep into his premisses (PM, vii). I study Russell's ideas as to how and why Frege's theories give rise to the paradoxes associated with set theory, and I connect Russell's diagnoses of the origins of the contradiction with the problems of ambiguity and identity examined in the previous chapters, problems which have both generated the problems and hidden them from view.

Predicates and the Appearance of Contradiction

One of the first clues as to what Russell believed was generating the contradiction appears in the letter in which Russell first announced the problem to Frege. There Russell wrote that he himself had originally agreed with Frege's theory in *Begriffsschrift*, §9, which states that in function-argument constructions, the function would be replaceable in the same way as signs standing for objects in such constructions were, but that this now seemed to him dubious because the following contradiction would then be derivable: "Let w be the predicate of being a predicate which cannot be predicated of itself. Can w be predicated of itself? From either answer follows its contradictory. We must therefore conclude that w is not a predicate.

Likewise, there is no class (as a whole) of those classes which, as wholes, are not members of themselves." (PMC, 130–31)

Ever lucid about the nature of predication, Frege was immediately able to shed some light on the source of problem. True to his convictions that the fundamental differences between predicates and objects are inviolate and founded in the deep nature of things (GB, 21–55), he immediately replied to Russell that the expression 'A predicate is predicated of itself' did not seem to him to be exact. "A predicate," Frege wrote to Russell upon hearing of the contradiction for the first time, "is as a rule a first level function which requires an object as argument and which cannot therefore have itself as argument (subject). Therefore I would rather say: 'A concept is predicated of its own extension'" (PMC, 132–33).

Frege had already struggled enough against language's propensity for confusing concepts and objects to understand that logical confusion might ensue if the basic differences between them were not respected, and a word for a concept were transformed into a name for an object and so were to come to be in a place for which it was not suited.[34] This was the dilemma he had so carefully spelled out in "On Concept and Object": "In logical discussions one often needs to say something about a concept, and to express this in the form usual for such predications . . . what is meant by the grammatical subject would be the concept; but the concept as such cannot play this part, in view of its predicative nature; it must first be converted into an object, or more precisely, an object must go proxy for it" (GB, 46). For Frege, predicates were by their very nature incomplete, and the words or symbols standing for them were unsaturated, in need of completion. For him, functions and concepts were special cases of predicates and contained a gap that was intended to receive a name for an object.

According to this characterization, predicates would in this respect be like containers, the essential difference between a predicate and object being like the difference between a container and what it contains. A container has an empty space intended for contents that may or may not be filled. And it could conceivably contain another container but it is absurd to think that a container might contain itself.

Analogously, if the relation of a class to its members is like the relationship of a club, a society, a community (or almost anything else said to have members) to its members, then it makes no more sense to talk of classes being members of themselves than it does to talk of anything else as being a member of itself. Clubs, societies, and communities may belong to another entity, but it is nonsensical to think of them as belonging to themselves.

If Frege was right about predication, and if the above two metaphors apply, then any statement that would assert of a concept, a function, or anything else essentially predicative in nature that it could take itself as an object would be itself absurd and contradictory; used as a premise in an argument, it would be bound to lead to absurd and contradictory conclusions. The contradiction brought Russell to share Frege's convictions in this regard.

Putting Symbols to Wrong Uses

The contradiction about classes that are not members of themselves had, in fact, made Russell keenly aware of the logical differences between predicates and names and ultimately obliged him to conclude that "the relation of a predicate to what it means is different from the relation of a name to what it means" (LK, 268). He was no longer prepared to state categorically, as he had in *The Principles of Mathematics* (§499), that predicates were individuals. It no longer seemed possible to him that a statement about x was generally analyzable into two parts, x and something said about x, both of which named independent entities with independent meanings of their own (EA, 137).

According to his new ideas, only particulars could be named. A predicate, by which he meant a word used to designate a quality such as red, white, square, or round, could never occur except as a predicate. What is predicative, he explained, suggests a structure, and no significant symbol can symbolize it in isolation. When a predicate "seems to occur as a subject, the phrase wants amplifying and explaining," he considered. Statements in which a predicate seems to be the subject have to be transformed into ones in which what is predicated is predicated. If this is not done, such sentences are liable to produce contradictions (LK, 205, 337-38).

Russell no longer believed there was a single concept of meaning but now thought there were "infinite numbers of different ways of meaning, i.e., different sorts of relation of the symbol to the symbolized, which are absolutely distinct" (LK, 268-69). In particular he had uncovered what he termed a "very unfortunate effect of the peculiarities of language" having to do with adjectives and relations. "All words are of the same logical type," he explained, "a word is a class of series, of noises or shapes according as it is heard or read. But the meanings of words are of various different types; an attribute (expressed by an adjective) is of a different type from the objects to which it can be (whether truly or falsely) attributed" (LK, 332). "For instance," he explained, "the word 'Socrates' . . . means a certain man; the word 'mortal' means a certain quality; and the sentence 'Socrates is mortal' means a certain fact. But these three sorts of meaning are entirely distinct, and you will get into the most hopeless contradictions if you think the word 'meaning' has the same meaning in each of these three cases" (LK, 186-87).

The contradictions had drawn Russell's attention to important fallacies that arise from not recognizing that there are different kinds of symbols and different kinds of relations between a symbol and what it symbolizes. When two words have two different types of meanings, the relations of the two words to what they stand for are also of different types, he now contended, and the failure to realize this was "a very potent source of error and confusion in philosophy" (LK, 333). The different sorts of symbols have different sorts of uses, and they must be kept always to the right use and not be put to the wrong use. The contradictions, he came to believe, all spring from fallacies produced by putting symbols to wrong uses. They "all arise from mistakes in symbolism, from putting one sort of symbol in the place where another sort of symbol ought to be," Russell wrote (LK, 185).

Russell's point can be illustrated by using different kinds of symbols to indicate the differences of logical type he came to believe in, a practice that transforms the contradictory outcome of Russell's reasoning as given in his first letter to Frege. Illegitimate substitution and false inference are now blocked by the difference in signs, making Russell's contradiction into:

W cannot be predicated of W, and W can be predicated of w

And the contradiction of the class of all those classes that are not members of themselves becomes:

Let W be the CLASS OF ALL THOSE CLASSES WHICH ARE NOT MEMBERS OF THEMSELVES. Then whatever class x may be, 'x is a W' is equivalent to 'x is not an x'. Hence giving to x the value w, 'w is a W' is equivalent to 'w is not a w' (re. LK, 59).

In other words, w is a member of the class W, and is not a member of itself for that would be nonsense. This is true in the case that w belongs to W, and it is not at all contradictory. The notation has set our reasoning straight, which, given our human propensity for error, is something we might hope our logic could do for us.

Considered in this way, Russell's paradoxes are not supplying us with contradictions, they are just faithfully telling us that: what is predicated of an object is of a different logical type from the object itself; the set X of x's is not is a member of what it is a set of; a concept is not an object; a property of an object is not equivalent to the object itself; a function is not an argument; what is incomplete is not complete; what is irreversible is not to be reversed; an adjective is not a noun; an intension is not an object. In short, logic is doing what logic is supposed to do.[35]

CONCEALED AMBIGUITY OF TYPE

In his quest to find out what was breeding the contradictions, Russell uncovered another phenomenon that masks differences of type and generates confusion by making it likely that false substitution will occur. The contradictions, he observed, all display a common characteristic which he described as self-reference or reflexiveness. "The appearance of contradiction," he wrote, "is always due to the presence of words embodying a concealed typical ambiguity, and the solution of the contradiction lies in bringing the concealed ambiguity to light" (PM, 65). He had found that:

> An indefinite number of contradictions . . . can easily be manufactured. . . . In all of them, the appearance of contradiction is produced by the presence of some word which has systematic ambiguity of type, such as *truth, falsehood, function, property, class, relation, cardinal, ordinal, name, definition.* Any such word, if its typical ambiguity is overlooked,

will apparently generate a totality containing members defined in terms of itself, and will thus give rise to vicious-circle fallacies. . . . [W]herever we have an illegitimate totality, a little ingenuity will enable us to construct a vicious circle fallacy leading to a contradiction, which disappears as soon as the typically ambiguous words are rendered typically definite, i.e. are determined as belonging to this or that type (PM, 64).

Russell defined a word having systematic ambiguity of type as one "having a strictly infinite number of meanings which it is important to distinguish" (LK, 268).

This ambiguity buried in natural languages has a particularly noxious effect within the context of Frege's and Russell's logic because, as Russell found, words and symbols having typical ambiguity "embrace practically all the ideas with which mathematics and mathematical logic are concerned. . . . [B]y employing typically ambiguous words and symbols we are able to make one chain of reasoning applicable to any one of an infinite number of different cases, which would not be possible if we were to forego the use of typically ambiguous words and symbols" (PM, 65). For example, according to Russell's analysis, Burali Forti's contradiction, the contradiction about the class of classes that are not members of themselves and all analogous contradictions were special cases of the following:

'Given a property ϕ and a function f, such that, if ϕ belongs to all the members of u, fu always exists, has the property ϕ, and is not a member of u; then the supposition that there is a class w of all terms having the property ϕ and that fw exists leads to the conclusion that fw both has and has not the property ϕ' (EA, 199, 153).

Symbols having systematic ambiguity occur in fifteen places in this two-sentence recipe for contradiction.

Logicians court contradiction when they reason with words that enjoy concealed typical ambiguity, — which look the same on the surface, but may ultimately be subject to logical rules other than the ones their outward appearance at first suggests. Where present in reasoning, superficial appearances make it easy for them to pass for what they are not, and so they can easily slip unnoticed from one logical place into another belonging to words of a different logical type, increasing the likelihood that self-referentiality and circularity of a paradox generating kind will occur. Impossible to distinguish by appearance alone, they can seem to be assertible, predicable of themselves until contradictions make it plain that they have sneaked into a place not suited to them. In this case Russell's discovery of the paradox made mathematicians stop short and search for a way to block the circularity.

The Vicious Circle Fallacy

"An analysis of the paradoxes to be avoided," Russell wrote while trying to escape them, "shows that they all result from a certain kind of vicious circle. The vicious circles in question all arise from supposing that a collection of objects may contain members which can only be defined by means of the collection as a whole" (PM, 37, 161; EA, 215). All the "contradictions have in common the assumption of a totality such that, if it were legitimate, it would at once be enlarged by new members defined in terms of itself" (LK, 63). They "arise where a phrase containing such words as *all* or *some* . . . appears itself to stand for one of the objects to which the words *all* or some are applied" (EA, 213), and "result from the fact that, according to current logical assumptions, there are what we may call *self-reproductive* processes and classes. That is, there are some properties such that, given any class of terms all having such a property, we can always define a new term also having the property in question. Hence we can never collect *all* the terms having the said property into a whole; because whenever we hope we have them all, the collection which we have immediately proceeds to generate a new term also having the said property" (EA, 144).

"In each contradiction something is said about *all* cases of some kind, and from what is said a new case seems to be generated, which both is and is not of the same kind as the cases of which *all* were concerned in what was said" (LK, 61).

In the case of the contradiction of the class of all classes that are not members of themselves, he argued, "if *all* classes, provided that they are not members of themselves, are members of w, this must also apply to w" (LK, 61). He reasoned that:

> In this case, the class w is defined by reference to 'all classes,' and then turns out to be one among classes. If we seek help by deciding that no class is a member of itself, then w becomes the class of all classes, and we have to decide that this is not a member of itself, i.e., is not a class. This is possible if there is no such thing as the class of all classes in the sense required by the paradox. That there is no such class results from the fact that, if suppose that there is, the supposition gives rise . . . to new classes lying outside the supposed total of all classes (LK, 62).

So to escape the contradiction, he felt obliged to conclude that:

> Whenever, by statements about "all" or "some" of the values that a variable can significantly take, we generate a new object, this new object must not be among the values which our previous variable could take, since, if it were, the totality of values over

which the variable could range would only be definable in terms of itself, and we should be involved in a vicious circle. For example, if I say "Napoleon had all the qualities that make a great general" I must define "qualities" in such a way that it will not include what I am now saying, i.e., "having all the qualities that make a great general" must not be itself a quality in the sense supposed (IMP, 189).

To avoid this vicious circle fallacy, he determined, we need a vicious circle principle, e.g., a principle stating that 'Whatever involves *all* of a collection must not be one of the collection' (LK, 63), or less exactly that 'Whatever involves *all* must not be one of the *all* which it involves' (EA, 204). This principle in turn leads to a theory of types that promised relief from the paradoxes.

The Vicious Circle Principle
and the Distinction of Logical Types

Early in his quest for a solution to the problem of the paradoxes, Russell had concluded that "the key to the whole mystery" would be found in the distinguishing of logical types (PofM, §104). Once having determined that the paradoxes arose "from the fact that an expression referring to *all* of some collection may itself appear to denote one of the collection," and having decided that "where this appears to occur, we are dealing with a false totality," Russell more fully developed a "doctrine of *types* of variables, proceeding on the principle that any expression which refers to *all* of some type must, if it denotes anything, denote something of a higher type than that to all of which it refers" (LK, 101).

His theory of the hierarchy of types promised to restore the logical structure forsaken when a normally predicative W is asserted of itself in statements of the form 'w is a w'. According to the theory, no totality of any kind could be a member of itself. Therefore, the totality of classes in the world could not be a class in the same sense in which a class is a class. A hierarchy of classes is established. The first type of classes is composed of classes made up entirely of particulars; the second type is composed of classes whose members are classes of the first type; the third type is composed of classes whose members are classes of the second type, and so on. The types obtained are mutually exclusive, making reflexive fallacies impossible and the notion of a class being a member of itself meaningless. Once such a hierarchy is established, a class of one type can never either be or not be identical to a class of another type.

"In this way," Russell maintained, "we obtain a series of types, such that, in all cases where formerly a paradox might have emerged, we now have a difference of type rendering the paradoxical statement meaningless" (EA, 201). By thus forbidding certain contradiction generating inferences, Russell pointed out, the classification of types "really performs the single, though essential, service of justifying us in refraining from entering on trains of reasoning which lead to contradictory conclusions" (PM, 24).

Russell thought the theory of types that he finally developed led "both to the avoidance of contradictions, and to the detection of the precise fallacy which has given rise to them" (PM, 1). And he believed that no solution to the contradictions was technically possible without it. However, he ultimately became aware that it was not "the key to the whole mystery." In his 1919 *Introduction to Mathematical Philosophy,* he would go so far as to concede that "the theory of types emphatically does not belong to the finished and certain part of our subject: much of the theory is inchoate and confused and obscure" (IMP, 135). He admitted that it was complicated and that all except its most general principles were uncertain. In particular, he said, it leads "to a more complete and radical atomism" than he had earlier believed possible (LK, 333). Quine has spelled out the fragmentation to which Russell was alluding. The theory of types, he explained,

> has unnatural and inconvenient consequences. Because the theory allows a class to have members only of uniform type, the universal class ∨ gives way to an infinite series of quasi-universal classes, one for each type. The negation $-x$ ceases to comprise all nonmembers of x, and comes to comprise only those nonmembers of x which are next lower in type than x. Even the null class ∧ gives way to an infinite series of null classes. The Boolean class algebra no longer applies to classes in general, but is reproduced rather within each type. The same is true of the calculus of relations. Even arithmetic, when introduced by definitions on the basis of logic, proves to be subject to the same reduplication. Thus the numbers cease to be unique; a new 0 appears for each type, likewise a new 1, and so on, just as in the case of ∨ and ∧. Not only are all these cleavages and reduplications intuitively repugnant, but they call continually for more or less elaborate technical maneuvers by way of restoring severed connections (FLPV, 91–92).

In addition, Russell recognized that the theory solved only some of the paradoxes for the sake of which he had invented it. Deeper problems caused the old contradiction to break out afresh, and he realized that "further subtleties" would be needed to solve them.

The theory of types restored some of the logical structure

Frege had eclipsed when talk of classes and their extensions had made him think that the irreversible relation of an object's falling under a concept could be turned into the reversible relation of identity and opened the door to the illegitimate inferences in the first place, but Russell's theory treats just the symptoms of the malady. The theory does not come to terms with the problem as to how and why the logical types had become confused in Frege's logic—as to what had made Frege try to obtain objects out of concepts in the first place. It does not adequately address the deeper logical problems concerning identity and substitutivity that had tempted Frege to introduce classes and a law saying that a class could be predicated of its own extension. The quest to uproot the paradoxes would require further investigations into what classes were.

Classes Away

Having evaded some of the contradictions by distinguishing between various types of objects, and having proposed a hierarchy of types, Russell took his ideas about logical type one step further and insisted most emphatically that classes could not be independent entities. Regarding them as such leads inescapably to the contradiction about the class of classes which are not members of themselves.

Russell had originally believed that: "When we say that a number of objects all have a certain property, we naturally suppose that the property is a definite object, which can be considered apart from any of all the objects, which have, or may be supposed to have, the property in question. We also naturally suppose that the objects which have the property form a *class*, and that the class is in some sense a new single entity, distinct, in general, from each member of the class" (EA, 163-64).

According to Frege's theory, Russell explained:

Whatever a class may be, it seems obvious that any propositional function ϕx determines a class, namely the class of objects satisfying ϕx. Thus 'x is human' defines the class of human beings, 'x is an even prime' defines the class whose only member is 2, and so on. We can then (so it would seem) define what we mean by 'x is a member of the class u', or 'x is a u' as we may say more shortly. This will mean: 'There is some function ϕ which defines the class u and is satisfied by x'. We then need an assumption to the effect that two functions define the same class when they are equivalent, i.e. such that for any value of x both are true or both false. Thus 'x is human' and 'x is featherless and two-legged' will define the same class. From this basis the whole theory of classes can be developed (EA, 171).

As he worked to finish the *Principles of Mathematics* in the wake of the paradoxes, Russell considered that the main problem with Frege's theory of classes had to do with the kind of entity his ranges were to be. Russell explained:

The reason which led me, against my inclination, to adopt an extensional view of classes, was the necessity of discovering some entity determinate for a given propositional function, and the same for any equivalent propositional function. Thus "x is a man" is equivalent (we will suppose) to "x is a featherless biped", and we wish to discover some one entity which is determined in the same way by both these propositional functions. The only single entity I have been able to discover is the class as one. (PofM, §486).

Any such object that might be proposed, he believed, presupposed the notion of class, i.e., an object uniquely determined by a propositional function, and equally determined by any equivalent propositional function (PofM, §489).

However, he had become convinced that this was precisely the kind of reasoning that had gotten himself, Frege, and others involved in the contradictions. For we cannot, then, escape the contradiction, Russell explained:

> For it is essential to an entity that it is a possible determination of x in any propositional function ϕx; that is, if ϕx is any propositional function, and a any entity, ϕa must be a significant expression. Now if a class is an entity, 'x is a u' will be a propositional function of u; hence, 'x is an x' must be significant. But if 'x is an x' is significant, the best hope of avoiding the contradiction is extinguished (EA, 171).

The solution to the paradoxes now seemed to Russell simply to lie in accommodating the fact that classes were not entities, or by merely abstaining from affirming that they were. There were no such things as classes and relations and functions as entities, he concluded, and the habit of talking of them was "merely a convenient abbreviation" (EA, 145, 200). The contradictions had persuaded him that "a property is not always an entity which can be detached from the argument of which it is asserted). . . . [P]roperties are not always (if ever) separable entities which can be put as arguments either to other properties or to themselves" (EA, 140). Likewise, functions could not always be considered independently of their arguments and do not always define classes. Standing alone, a propositional function "may be taken to be a mere schema, an empty shell, an

empty receptacle for meaning, not something already significant" (IMP, 157).

The idea that classes were not entities shed light on the
ontological nature of classes by saying what they were not, but
Russell had to do more than that. To avoid the contradictions he
decided he would have to devise a technique for making classes
vanish from the reasoning in which they were present. He would
have to provide a way of interpreting ordinary statements about
classes without assuming they were entities, construct a theory
that would actually show them to be mere *façons de parler,* and
void of any independent reality. Analogies he was able to draw
between descriptions and classes as incomplete symbols that
do not designate entities and the success he had with his 1905
theory of definite descriptions finally gave him an idea as to how
classes might be analyzed away much as descriptions had been.

9

Russell's Paradoxes and His Theory of Definite Descriptions

Bertrand Russell always said that his theory of definite descriptions represented his first breakthrough in his efforts to find a solution to the paradoxes associated with set theory.[36] The theory, he considered, had "swept away a host of otherwise insoluble problems."[37]

Like Frege, Russell connected certain problems encountered in trying to translate descriptions into the logical idiom their theories required with the set-theoretical paradoxes. Frege originally thought that descriptions like 'the discoverer of America' or 'the extension of the word 'star'' denoted objects, and his Basic Law V would have made such descriptions subject to the same formal rules of identity as those governing objects, and so amenable to extensional treatment and substitution. But Frege ultimately condemned that operation as illicit, and he finally judged his reliance on it as having been the fatal flaw in his logic: the source of the paradoxes of set theory that he considered had "dealt the death blow to set theory itself" (PW, 269). Russell's paradox, he said, had finally led him to conclude that, although the definite article creates the impression that such descriptions name objects, there were in fact no objects for which such descriptions could be linguistically appropriate designations (PW, 269-70).

Once the paradoxes of set theory had put an end to the logical honeymoon Russell was having when he began writing the *Principles of Mathematics,* and once he had "settled down to a resolute attempt to find a solution of the paradoxes,"[38] he devoted almost all his time to denoting problems[39] that he thought were probably relevant to his problems with the contradictions. The success he finally had in analyzing away descriptions in his 1905 article "On Denoting" proved to him that denoting was indeed relevant, and the theory of definite descriptions he expounded in the article would go on to play a crucial role in *Principia Mathematica* (PM, chapter 3, *14, *20), a work specially framed to solve the paradoxes troubling students of symbolic logic and the theory of aggregates (PM, 1).

Although Frege and Russell both established connections between the logical behavior of descriptions and the set-theoretical paradoxes, the precise nature of the relation they perceived is not as apparent as one might like it to be. So it is important to examine how comprehending the logic of descriptions might have helped Russell to unlock the mystery of the paradoxes.

Incomplete Symbols

Russell's decision to develop a procedure for analyzing away classes modeled after his way of handling descriptions as incomplete symbols was a major breakthrough in his efforts to unlock the mystery of contradictions arising from treating incomplete symbols as if they stood for objects. The contradiction about the classes that are not members of themselves had convinced him that one could not generally suppose that objects which all have a certain property form a class that is in some sense a new entity distinct from the objects making it up. Unbridled use of the principle of abstraction—according to which, given a particular condition upon y, there would be a class x which was an independent entity whose members were just those objects y fulfilling that condition—was producing false abstractions, pseudo-objects, which were in turn causing the contradictions or paradoxes. Russell had been brought to the point of writing of classes that: "It becomes very difficult to see what they can be, if they are to be more than symbolic fictions. And if we can find any way of dealing with them as symbolic fictions, we increase the logical security of our position, since we avoid the need of assuming that there are classes without being compelled to make the opposite assumption that there are no classes" (IMP, 184).

Certain similarities Russell had observed between classes and descriptions suggested to him that his theory of definite descriptions might hold the secret to this "logical security." The analogies were compelling enough to make him ready to relegate symbols for classes to the same status as expressions designating predicates, concepts, functions, properties, and descriptions, which he also considered to be incomplete and meaningless in isolation. It now seemed to him that "Classes, relations, numbers, and indeed almost all the things mathematics deals with, are 'false abstractions' in the sense in which 'the present King of England', or 'the present King of France' is a false abstraction. . . . Language which speaks about classes is, in fact, merely a form of short-hand, and becomes illegitimate as soon as it is incapable of translation into language which says nothing about classes" (EA, 166).

Denoting puzzles had shown Russell that the "first thing to realize about a definite description is that it is not a name . . . a simple symbol used to designate a certain particular or by extension an object" (LK, 244). Upon close inspection, Russell had found that descriptions which at first blush appear to designate an object that might conform to the conventional behavior expected of objects in seemingly normal substitution legitimizing identity statements do not actually do so. "A proposition containing a description," he came to insist, "was not identical with what that proposition becomes when a name is substituted, even if the name names the same object as the description describes" (IMP, 174).

Letting oneself be misled by grammar into thinking that incomplete symbols could be treated as if they represented independent entities and an "entire delusion" and had been the source of "a great deal of confusion and false philosophy," Russell concluded (LK, 253). But, statements containing descriptions had proven amenable to further analysis. So once Russell had determined that classes and descriptions both fell into the same logical category of non-entities represented by incomplete symbols, the twin requirement of eluding the paradoxes and of satisfying the logical exigencies that had originally obliged Frege to resort to classes led Russell to consider that proper logical analysis might show how, though void of meaning in isolation symbols for classes, like descriptions, might be significant in context. Russell came to believe: "It is absolutely necessary, if a statement about a class is to be significant and not pure nonsense, that it should be capable of being translated into a form in which it does not mention the class at all. . . . It is analogous to what I was saying about descriptions: the symbol for a class is an incomplete symbol; it does not really stand for part of the propositions in which symbolically it occurs, but in the right analysis of those propositions that symbol has been broken up and disappeared" (LK, 262). Russell now had a concrete idea as to how he might break the vicious circle of the class paradoxes and sweep his problems away. He would extend his ideas about ridding reasoning of descriptions to include class symbols. He reasoned:

> We cannot accept "class" as a primitive idea. We must seek a definition on the same lines as the definition of descriptions, i.e. a definition which will assign a meaning to propositions in whose verbal

or symbolic expression words or symbols apparently representing classes occur, but which will assign a meaning that altogether eliminates all mention of classes from a right analysis of such propositions. We shall then be able to say that the symbols for classes are mere conveniences, not representing objects called "classes," and that classes are in fact, like descriptions, logical fictions, or (as we say) "incomplete symbols" (IMP, 181–82).

The contradictions were, however, a distressing aftereffect of introducing the extensions Frege had reluctantly appealed to because he saw that, without them, the theory of identity and substitutivity he was prescribing could produce nonsensical conclusions or be sterile and unproductive (FA, §66–67). Frege had resorted to extensions out of necessity, and they served a definite purpose in his system.

Russell also was well aware of the need for classes. In the closing pages of the *Principles of Mathematics,* he wrote: "The final conclusion . . . is that the class as one, or the whole composed of the terms of the class, is probably a genuine entity" (PofM, §492). He explained that "without a single object to represent an extension, Mathematics crumbles. Two propositional functions which are equivalent for all values of the variable may not be identical, but it is necessary there should be some object determined by both. Any object that may be proposed, however, presupposes the notion of *class* . . . an object uniquely determined by a propositional function, and determined equally by any equivalent propositional function" (PofM, §489).

So Russell could not very well just demolish classes. The trick was to find a way of making them disappear without completely letting go of them. And his new technique for analyzing away descriptions made him see how this might actually be accomplished. Confident that his theory of definite descriptions had blazed the trail, Russell set out to devise a way "to show that the incomplete symbols which we introduce as representatives of classes yield all the propositions for the sake of which classes might be thought essential. When this has been shown," he believed, "the mere principle of economy leads to the nonintroduction of classes except as incomplete symbols" (PM, 72).

If all went according to his new plan, classes would have a meaning in context and function as parts of significant phrases, without having to exist. The theory of classes of *Principia Mathematica,* (*20) would provide a notation to represent classes while avoiding "the assumption that there are such things as classes . . . by merely defining propositions in whose expression the symbols representing the classes occur, just as, in *14, we defined propositions containing descriptions" (PM, 187).

Having Classes and Deleting Them Too

To "lay hold upon the extension of a concept," Frege had proposed transforming "a sentence in which mutual subordination is asserted of concepts into a sentence expressing an identity." Since only objects could figure in identity statements, he realized he would have to find a way of correlating objects and concepts in a way that correlated mutually subordinate concepts with the same object. He suggested this might be achieved by translating language that asserts mutual subordination into statements of the form 'the extension of the concept X is the same as the extension of the concept Y' in which the descriptions would then be regarded as proper names as indicated by the presence of the definite article. By permitting such a transformation, he acknowledged, one is conceding that such proper names have meanings (PW, 181–82).

It was precisely that sort of recipe for making what was incomplete behave as if it were complete in identity statements that Russell's paradox had cast doubt upon. And the problems that procedure caused were precisely the ones Russell hoped to circumvent through his new theory of classes based on the theory of definite descriptions, by which he hoped he might actually realize Frege's goal of correlating classes with extensions in such a way that concepts that are mutually subordinate would be correlated with the same objects (GB, 214).

According to Russell's theory of definite descriptions: "There is a term c such that ϕx is always equivalent to 'x is c'" (IMP, 178). That being so, the putative identity statement 'Scott is the author of *Waverley*' might be rewritten 'Scott wrote *Waverley*; and it is always true of c that if c wrote *Waverley*, c is identical with Scott' (LK, 55). In this construal of the sentence, what was not identical has been made to be equivalent. A symbol deemed equatable with 'Scott' has gone proxy for the description, and this symbol will generally be "obedient to the same formal rules of identity as symbols which directly represent objects" (PM, 83). So the truth value of a great many statements that are naturally made about the definite description will be unaffected by the analysis.[40]

This means of drawing objects out of descriptions provided Russell with a practical model of how to make non-entities function as entities without incurring contradictory results. Unadulterated class abstraction was generating contradictions, but the theory of definite descriptions was a different way of making an object fit to go proxy for what was said about it. By adapting the theory to class symbols, he thought one might acquire a "method of obtaining an extensional function from any given function of a function," which was precisely what the theory of classes needed (PM, 187). A theory of classes modeled after the theory of definite descriptions could stipulate that for a class determined by the function ϕx and having the property f, there would be a function having the property *f* which was formally equivalent to ϕx (IMP, 188). This, Russell considered, "gives a meaning to any statement about a class which can be made significantly about a function; and it will be found that technically it yields the results which are required in order to make a theory symbolically satisfactory" (IMP, 188).

Whenever a symbol for a class or a description appeared to be designating an object, Russell would redefine it in terms of primitive ideas already on hand (PM, 24, 30). Analyzed in this way, purely logical structures could be substituted for classes without any apparent ill effect. By thus replacing constructions out of known entities for inferences to unknown entities, statements in which classes appear to be mentioned could be interpreted without actually supposing that there were classes (LK, 326–27). However, though the class symbols might well "have no meaning in isolation, yet those of their formal properties with which we have been hitherto concerned are the same as the corresponding properties of symbols which have a meaning in isolation" (PM, 198, 196). Russell was satisfied that though the real meaning of the notation ultimately adopted was very complicated, it nevertheless had "an apparently simple meaning which, except at certain crucial points, can without danger be substituted in thought for the real meaning" (PM, 1).

But displaying substitution behavior queer enough to make Russell realize that they were unfit to do duty in identity statements without undergoing some sort of extra logical treatment was not all that symbols for classes and definite descriptions had in common. Russell also realized that resolving the paradoxes would mean coming to terms with problems with classes caused by the fact that it was "quite self-evident that equivalent propositional functions are often not identical" (PofM, §500), and these problems display certain formal similarities with the puzzles about descriptions that had impressed on Russell the need to remove descriptions from statements in which they were present in the first place.

One of the reasons Russell had had to find a way to get rid of descriptions was that, while an informative statement of the form 'the author of *Waverley* is the author of *Marmion*' could be true and seem to be a genuine identity statement in virtue of the fact that both descriptions were true of the same individual, the two descriptions were obviously not themselves identical, nor were they always intersubstitutable salva veritate. If the only thing that mattered were that both descriptions are true of the same person, Russell observed, then any other phrase true of Scott would yield the same statement. Then 'Scott is the author of *Marmion*' would be the same as 'Scott is the author of *Waverley*', which is obviously not so, because from the one we learn that Scott wrote *Marmion* and from the other that he wrote *Waverley*, but the former statement tells us nothing about *Waverley* and the latter nothing about *Marmion*. Properly re-construed, the descriptions would disappear and the statement transformed into: 'Someone wrote *Waverley* and no one else did, and that someone else wrote *Marmion* and no one else did'.[41]

This way of correlating mutually subordinate descriptions with the same object could help solve a parallel problem in the paradox plagued theory of classes, e.g., the problem of two propositional functions having the same graph without every-thing that is true of one being true of the other. For just as de-scriptions are tied to a particular characterization of an object, so classes are formed by specifying the definite property giving the class. Moreover, just as two different descriptions might be true of the same object, so a single class of objects might be defined in different ways, each one corresponding to a different sense of the class name. Yet as Russell observed "if a and b be different class-concepts such that $x \in a$ and $x \in b$ are equivalent for all values of x, the class-concept under which a falls and nothing else will not be identical with that under which falls *b* and nothing else" (PofM, §488).

Russell was pleased to point out, however, that the theory of classes inspired by his theory of descriptions would leave intact all the fundamental properties desired of classes, the principal one of these being that "two classes are identical when, and only when, their defining functions are formally equivalent" (PM, 189). "The incomplete symbols which take the place of classes serve the purpose of technically providing something identical in the case of two functions having the same extension," he believed (PM, 187). By virtue of his new theory of classes as incomplete symbols, he said: "You find that, all the formal properties that you desire of classes, all their formal uses in mathematics, can be obtained without supposing for a moment that there are such things as classes, without supposing, that is to say, that a proposition in which symbolically a class occurs, does in fact contain a constituent corresponding to that symbol, and when rightly analysed that symbol will disappear, in the same sort of way as descriptions disappear when the propositions are rightly analysed in which they occur" (LK, 266; PM, chapter 3).

The theory of classes set out in *Principia Mathematica* (which relies heavily on the axiom of reducibility discussed below) would sweep away the contradiction about the class of classes that are not members of themselves because by it, Russell stated:

> [A] proposition about a class is always to be reduced
> to a statement about a function which defines the
> class, *i.e.* about a function which is satisfied by the
> members of the class and by no other arguments.
> Thus a class is an object derived from a function
> and presupposing the function. . . . Hence a class
> cannot, by the vicious-circle principle, significantly
> be the argument to its defining function. . . . Hence

a class neither satisfies nor does not satisfy its defining function, and therefore . . . is neither a member of itself nor not a member of itself. . . . Thus
if α is a class, the statement "α is not a member
of α" is always meaningless, and there is therefore
no sense in the phrase "the class of those classes
which are not members of themselves." Hence the
contradiction which results from supposing there is
such a class disappears (PM, 62–63).

Presto chango! By an act of logical prestidigitation, the theory
of classes has been rendered "symbolically satisfactory." We
can have our classes and delete them too. Statements verbally
concerned with classes have been reduced to statements that
are concerned with propositions and propositional functions.
Logicians can effectively pass from a class to its extension on
paper without incurring contradictory results. We have avoided
contradictions arising from supposing that classes are entities
and acquired a technique for laying hold of the extension of a
class. In addition, functions having the same extension would
be identical. And our efforts have brought us ever nearer to the
deep reasons why Frege's introducing extensions into his logic
caused the paradoxes in the first place.

The Ultimate Source of the Contradictions

Russell considered his technique for making incomplete symbols obey the same formal rules of identity as symbols that
directly represent objects to be a breakthrough in solving the
paradoxes and a host of other problems. However, he realized that incomplete symbols could obey only the same formal
rules of identity as symbols referring to objects in so far as "we
only consider the *equivalence* of the resulting variable (or constant) values of propositional functions and not their identity"

(PM, 83), an observation which brings us right back to the problems concerning logical abstraction, identity, and substitutivity, which first obliged Frege to introduce extensions.

So to assess the ultimate effectiveness of the various techniques Russell invented for evading the paradoxes, it is important to look closely at what Russell once called the "ultimate source" of the contradictions. Russell once wrote that the cause of his and Burali-Forti's contradiction was to be found in that: "If x and y are identical, ϕx implies ϕy. This holds in each particular case, but we cannot say it holds *always*, because the various particular cases have not enough in common. This distinction is difficult and subtle. . . . The neglect of it is the ultimate source of all the contradictions which have hitherto beset the theory of the transfinite" (EA, 188). Russell's statement brings us all the way back to Frege's original idea that "the existence of different names for the same content is the very heart of the matter if each is associated with a different way of determining the content" (BS, §8), and to his original reasons for introducing extensions.

Once we have an informative identity statement, we can, in fact, easily illustrate Russell's point by generating contradictions by fashioning statements out of the piece of information our informative statement conveys, and, by virtue of which, it is informative and not a mere tautology. For example, someone believing that statements flanked by a description are genuine identities that can serve as paradigms of informative identity statements might turn to Quine's paradigm of a true identity statement:

'9 is the number of the planets',

which for them has the logical form '$x = y$'. The 1930 discovery that there were nine, not eight planets constituted a valuable extension of scientific knowledge about the universe that could not have been established a priori (re. GB, 56). Ever since this important astronomical discovery was made, schoolchildren have been taught that the statement was true. If it is indeed a true identity, then translated into Frege's and Russell's class talk, astronomers have discovered that 9 belongs to the same class as the number of the planets does, and since the number of the planets belongs to the class of all those things which are 9, class A = class B.

However, the number of the planets also belongs to the class C of all those things discoverable by astronomical observation (FLPV, 21). And by substitution we have:

y belongs to C
x = y
Therefore, x belongs to C.

But, taking Quine as our authority, 9 does not belong to the class of all those things discoverable by astronomical observation.

Therefore, x does not belong to C.

And we have our contradiction.

For those who are rightly skeptical as to whether descriptions belong in identity statements at all, we might look at the simpler case in which x = y in virtue of the fact that 'x' and 'y' are two names for the same object. For example, in an attempt to uncover tax evaders, President Kim of South Korea has decreed that all bank accounts must be registered in the owner's true name for, apparently, many Koreans hold accounts under false names for purposes of tax evasion.

Suppose that South Korean citizen x holds two bank accounts, one under his true name and another under the false name 'y'. Since 'x' and 'y' are two names for the same South Korean citizen, 'x = y' is a true statement. However, although 'x' and 'y' designate the same person, they will not be interchangeable because they determine that person in different ways, lead to him from different directions—which is precisely why the tax evader has used two names to begin with. In particular, in addition to naming the tax evader, 'x' names someone holding an account under a true name, but y's account is under a false name. And it is this fact that marks the difference between an honest and a dishonest citizen. So translated into class talk we have:

> x belongs to the class A of all people holding accounts under their true names
> x = y
> Therefore, y belongs to class A.

But we know that 'y' designates someone who holds an account that is not under his or her true name, so:

> Therefore, y does not belong to class A.

And we have our contradiction. The more informative an identity statement is, the more potentially truth value disturbing predicates can intervene to wreck substitutivity. And the more potential there is to reach contradictory and paradoxical conclusions. And that is the heart of the matter.

The following example points up the difficulty: Say that A is the class of all those holding account 1, and B is the class of all those holding account 2. Now, x has account 1 under her true name and account 2 under a false name, so that while $x \in A$, and $x \in B$ are equivalent for all values of x, there will be many contexts in which the holder of account 1 will not be interchangeable with the holder of account 2. Even though we clearly have a single object determined equally by a set of equivalent functions, we cannot assume that two functions define the same class when they are equivalent, i.e., that for any value of x both are true or both false. Though 'x belongs to the class of all those holding account 1' and 'x belongs to the class of those holding account 2', many things which are true of account holder 1 will not be true of account holder 2, and vice versa. Evading this particular problem about identity would require more drastic measures.

THE AXIOM OF REDUCIBILITY

The contradictions most intimately concerned with identity and the formal equivalence of functions proved especially hard to stamp out. For these, Russell had to develop a new tactic aimed more directly at the theory of identity that had brought about the confusion of types and the reification of incomplete symbols in the first place.

In particular, Russell still faced the following predicament: The contradictions had taught him that there was a hierarchy of logical types and that it was a fallacy to allow a sign standing for an object belonging to one logical type to be substituted for a sign standing for an object belonging to another type. And it could "be proved impossible to speak of *all* the propositional functions that can have arguments of a given type" (IMP, 185). If contradiction producing vicious circle fallacies were to be avoided, functions would have to be divided into types, and all talk of functions would then necessarily be limited to some one type. The vicious circle principle would effectively make statements about all functions true with a given argument, or all properties of a some given object, meaningless.

Russell was perfectly aware, however, that "it is not difficult to show that the various functions which can take a given object a as argument are not all of one type" (IMP, 189), and, even "that the functions which can take a given argument are of an infinite series of types" (IMP, 190). By various technical devices we could, he explains, "construct a variable which would run through the first n of these types, where n is finite, but we cannot construct a variable which will run through them all, and, if we could, that mere fact would at once generate a new type of function with the same arguments, and would set the whole process going again" (IMP, 190). So whatever selection of functions one makes there will always be other functions that will not be included in the selection.

Russell moreover realized that "it must be possible to make propositions about *all* the classes that are composed of individuals, or about *all* the classes that are composed of objects of any one logical 'type.'" If this were not the case, many uses of classes would go astray" (IMP, 185). "If mathematics is to be possible," he believed, "it is absolutely necessary . . . that we should have some method of making statements which will usually be equivalent to what we have in mind when we (inaccurately) speak of 'all properties of x.' . . . Hence we must find, if possible, some method of reducing the order of a propositional function without affecting the truth or falsehood of its values" (PM, 166; LK, 80).

So to cope with contradictions arising from necessary talk of all properties, or all functions, Russell introduced the axiom of reducibility. This specially designed axiom would be "equivalent to the assumption that 'any combination or disjunction of predicates is equivalent to a single predicate'" (EA, 250; PM, 58–59) and would provide a way of dealing with any function of a particular argument by means of some formally equivalent function of a particular type. It would thus yield most of the results that would otherwise require recourse to the problematical notions of all functions or all properties, and so legitimize a great mass of reasoning apparently dependent on such notions (PM, 56).

For Russell, the axiom embodied all that was essential in his theory of classes (IMP, 191; PM, 58). "By the help of the axiom of reducibility," Russell affirmed, "we find that the usual properties of classes result. For example, two formally equivalent functions determine the same class, and conversely, two functions which determine the same class are formally equivalent" (EA, 248–49). He now believed classes themselves to be useful mainly as a technical means of achieving what the axiom of reducibility would effect (IMP, 191). And it seemed to him "that the sole purpose which classes serve, and one main reason which makes them linguistically convenient, is that they provide a method of reducing the order of a propositional function" (PM, 166). Classes were producing contradictions. Thus they should be expunged and replaced with this axiom that seemed to him "to be the essence of the usual assumption of classes" and to retain "as much of classes as we have any use for, and little enough to avoid the contradictions which a less grudging admission of classes is apt to entail" (PM, 166–67; LK, 82; IMP, 191).

Russell leans on the axiom of reducibility at every crucial point in his definition of classes in *Principia Mathematica* (75–81). He considered that many of the proofs of *Principia* "become fallacious when the axiom of reducibility is not assumed, and in some cases new proofs can only be obtained with with considerable labour" (PM, xliii); "many propositions which are nearly indubitable can be deduced from it, and no equally plausible way is known by which these propositions could be true if the axiom were false" (EA, 251).

Moreover, Russell believed that without the axiom, or its equivalent, one would be compelled to regard identity as indefinable and to admit that two objects might agree in all their predicates without being identical (PM, 58). In particular, by resorting to the axiom of reducibility one might avoid a difficulty with the definition of identity that Russell explained as follows:

> We might attempt to define "x is identical with y" as meaning "whatever is true of x is true of y," *i.e.,* "ϕx always implies ϕy." But here, since we are concerned to assert all values of "ϕx implies ϕy" re-

garded as a function of ϕ, we shall be compelled to impose upon ϕ some limitation which will prevent us from including among values of ϕ values in which "all possible values of ϕ" are referred to. Thus for example "x" is identical with "a" is a function of x; hence, if it is a legitimate value of ϕ in "ϕx always implies ϕy," we shall be able to infer, by means of the above definition, that if x is identical with a, and x is identical with y, then y is identical with a. Although the conclusion is sound, the reasoning embodies a vicious-circle fallacy, since we have taken "$(\phi) \cdot \phi x$ implies ϕa" as a possible value of ϕx, which it cannot be. If, however, we impose any limitation upon ϕ, it may happen, so far as appears at present, that with other values of ϕ we might have ϕx true and ϕy false, so that our proposed definition of identity would plainly be wrong (PM, 49).

So the axiom would have the effect of legitimizing statements of identity based on the notion of having all properties in common, and Russell thought of it as a generalized form of Leibniz's principle of the identity of indiscernibles (IMP, 192; PM, 57; EA, 242). Without it, or its equivalent, he considered, one could not be sure that x and y were identical if for all values of ϕ, ϕx implied ϕy. For by the vicious circle principle, statements about all values of ϕ were inadmissible.

"But in virtue of the axiom of reducibility," Russell writes in *Principia Mathematica* *13, "it follows that, if $x = y$ and x satisfies ψx, where ψ is any function . . . then y also satisfies ψy." And this effectively made his definition of identity as powerful as if he had been able to appeal to all functions of x (PM, 168). For if one assumes the axiom of reducibility, then "every property belongs to the same collection of objects as is defined by some predicate. Hence there is some predicate common and peculiar to the objects which are identical with *x*. This predicate belongs to *x*, since *x* is identical with itself; hence it belongs to *y*, since *y* has all the predicates of *x*; hence *y* is identical with *x*. It follows that we may *define x* and *y* as identical when all the predicates of *x* belong to *y*" (PM, 57; EA, 243). And this makes many kinds of general statements possible that would otherwise involve vicious circle paradoxes (EA, 249).

So by virtue of the axiom of reducibility, one might have the properties of identity and substitutivity on which the logic of *Principia Mathematica* is built. And, as Quine has pointed out, the axiom actually "has the effect of reinstating the whole platonistic logic of classes" (FLPV, 127), "guarantees outright the dispensability of the ramified theory,"[42] and "implies the superfluousness of the very distinctions that give it substance."[43] In other words, Russell was finally back to square one, i.e., to the reasons why Frege's theory of identity of substitutivity had made him appeal to extensions in the first place.

Yet, in spite of all that might be achieved by means this axiom, Russell expressed reservations about it reminiscent of those Frege had had regarding Basic Law V, which would have accomplished the same thing. Russell deemed his axiom "only convenient, not necessary" (IMP, 192), and even called it "a dubious assumption" (IMP, 193). He said that he did not "see any reason to believe that the axiom of reducibility is logically necessary," and that "the admission of this axiom into a system of logic is therefore a defect, even if the axiom is empirically true" (IMP, 193). "This axiom," he admitted, "has a purely pragmatic justification: it leads to the desire results, and to no others. But clearly it is not the sort of axiom with which we can rest content" (PM, xiv).

But what had made such a measure necessary?

The axiom of reducibility was another attempt to rub out the difference between equality and identity. In his search for a criterion for deciding whether in all cases x is the same as y, Frege had turned to Leibniz's principle of substitutivity of identicals (FA, §65). Then he adopted a form of expression by which being the same in one way would be the same as being the same in all ways, making the difference between equality and identity go away. After that, he reluctantly introduced extensions as a way of artificially rectifying the problems with substitutivity that the attempt to equate equality and identity had caused (FA, §§66-67). Basic Law V would guarantee that an identity holding between two concepts could be transformed into an identity of extensions and conversely, that functions having the same extensions were identical—and it leads to Russell's paradox.

Russell struggled with the ambiguities concealed in Frege's theory of identity, and he devised some sharp logical instruments to exorcise or subjugate the intensions marking the difference between equality and identity which had not vanished from reasoning as obligingly as hoped. Wielding his theory of types and his technique for analyzing away classes, Russell began sweeping away the tangled web Frege began to weave when he violated common sense by adopting the inference wrecking practice of identifying identity with lesser forms of equivalence. By adroitly wiping out a wealth of intensions and casting them into logical oblivion, the axiom of reducibility would sweep *Principia Mathematica* nearly clean of intensions and so win new territory for extensional ontology—except in certain contumnacious cases where intensions appear again in propria persona.

10

Propositional Attitudes

The logical landscape of *Principia Mathematica* and related systems was predetermined never to be able to deal adequately with intensions. However, some phenomena that defied translation into an extensional idiom right from the beginning are still found lurking about today to blur the clean shaven, austere picture of reality Russell was so eager to bequeath posterity. Notorious among these are what Russell called propositional attitudes. He considered the problems raised by them to be crucial (PM, 401-02).

Propositional attitudes are expressions involving notions — like believing, supposing, asserting, and denying — which govern whole clauses or statements. They often figure in accounts of human mental activities, but this is by no means exclusively the case, and it is easy to find other examples of statements exhibiting the same kind of problematic, non-extensional behavior in other realms of inquiry. Frege, the pioneer in the subject, gave as examples subordinate clauses introduced by words like 'say', 'hear', 'be of the opinion', 'be convinced', 'conclude', 'it seems that...', 'It seems to me that...', 'I think that...', 'to be pleased', 'to regret', 'to approve', 'to blame', 'to hope', 'command that', 'ask that', 'forbid that', 'to fear', 'doubt whether', 'not to know what', 'know', 'discover', 'it is known that' (GB, 66-68, 76). His list is clearly not exhaustive, but it suffices to show that propositional attitudes are abundant and play a significant enough role in philosophical and scientific discourse not to be dismissed offhandedly.

"There is an absolute gulf," Russell warned in an appendix to *Principia Mathematica*, "between the assertion of a proposition and an assertion about the proposition" (PM, 408). "When an assertion occurs," he explained, "it is made by means of a particular fact, which is an instance of the proposition asserted. But this particular fact is, so to speak, 'transparent', nothing is said about it, but by means of it something is said about something else. It is this 'transparent' quality which belongs to propositions as they occur in truth-functions" (PM, 407). However, he emphasized, "the p that occurs when we assert p, and the p that occurs in 'A asserts p' are by no means identical" (PM, 408).

And, Russell himself once inadvertently provided an excellent example of precisely the gulf he was alluding to when he wrote in a letter to Frege: "I believe that $(4^2 - 3^2 = 7) \cdot = \cdot (7 = 7)$ is false" (PMC, 170). If Russell really believed this, his statement is true. However, it is clearly not truth functional because the truth or falsehood of the statement as a whole no longer depends on the truth or falsehood of its component parts. In such propositional attitude contexts, the p that occurs when p itself is asserted, and the p that occurs when something is asserted of p no longer exhibit the same logical behavior. In particular, they are no longer interchangeable salva veritate; interchanging them, we actually risk reversing the truth value of our statements or producing outright nonsense . . . bringing a host of problems to logic as conceived by Frege, Russell, and those who would further their insights.

Frege Spots the Problem

Frege confessed several times that he had engaged in a serious battle about introducing extensions. And the views expounded in his famous 1892 article "On Sense and Reference," where the propositional attitudes problem was first discussed, were surely conceived while he was actually waging his personal war with extensionality. Extensions won the day, and by the time his *Basic Laws of Arithmetic* was published in 1893, Frege was able to say that though his decision would not please everyone, extensions had acquired "great fundamental importance" in his work, and he could not see how he could do without them (BL, vii–xi).

However, Frege was perfectly lucid about both the significance and the dangers for his logic of discourse that would not be translated into his extensional idiom. He specifically addressed the problem in "On Sense and Reference," where he acknowledged that were his views on truth functionality correct, then in accordance with Leibniz's principle that two things are the same as each other, of which one can be substituted for the other salva veritate, the truth value of a sentence "must remain unchanged when an expression is replaced by an expression with the same reference" (GB, 64), and "the truth value of a sentence containing another as part must remained unchanged when the part is replaced by another sentence having the same truth-value" (GB, 65).

Frege saw, though, that there were many cases in which a part of a sentence could not be simply replaced by another having the same truth value without altering the thought and harming the truth of the sentence as a whole (GB, 65–78). In making such substitutions the truth value might actually be reversed (PMC, 153–54). In particular, he was aware that parts of sentences governed by propositional attitudes constituted an obvious exception to this rule. A good illustration of how propositional attitudes can wreak extensional havoc is Russell's statement:

"I believe that $(4^2 - 3^2 = 7) \cdot = \cdot (7 = 7)$ is false"
(PMC, 170).

Taken out of the propositional attitude context, the equation whose falsehood Russell is affirming would normally be a paradigm of a true statement. And to say that it is false, as Russell has, would be to make a false statement. Once placed within the purview of a propositional attitude, however, the customary truth value of the components of that false statement no longer have any bearing on the truth or falsehood of Russell's declaration as a whole. For, taking Russell at his word, we are obliged to acknowledge that his statement is true, i.e., it is true that he believes that a certain true equation is false. Russell's statement as a whole is true and plainly not truth functional. A clause or another part of the sentence having equal truth value may not always be substituted for one another in the sentence, Frege explained, because it expresses more through its connection with the propositional attitude than it does in isolation (GB, 76).

FREGE'S EXPLANATION

In "On Sense and Reference," Frege also sought to uncover "the essential reasons why a subordinate clause may not always be replaced by another of equal truth value without harm to the truth of the whole sentence structure" (GB, 77). Our signs, he theorized there, both express a sense and designate a reference (GB, 61). When two different signs designate the same reference, they are normally interchangeable salva veritate. However, Frege observed, "$a = a$ and $a = b$ are obviously statements of differing cognitive value; $a = a$ holds a priori . . . while statements of the form $a = b$ often contain very valuable extensions of our knowledge and cannot always be established a priori" (GB, 56). "The explanation," he concludes, "is that for the purpose of knowledge, the sense of the sentence, viz., the thought expressed by it, is no less relevant that its reference, i.e. its truth value" (GB, 78).

Propositional attitude contexts produce a bifurcation in the meaning of the words in the subordinate clause, bringing these senses of the words suddenly to the fore. Then, Frege explained:

The words have their indirect reference, coincident with what is customarily their sense. . . . It is indifferent to the truth of the whole whether the subordinate clause is true or false. Let us compare, for instance, the two sentences 'Copernicus believed that the planetary orbits are circles' and 'Copernicus believed that the apparent motion of the sun is produced by the real motion of the Earth.' One subordinate clause can be substituted for the other without harm to the truth. The main clause and the subordinate clause together have as their sense only a single thought, and the truth of the whole includes neither the truth nor the untruth of the subordinate clause. In such cases it is not permissible to replace one expression in the subordinate clause by another having the same customary reference, but only by one having the same indirect reference, i.e. the same customary sense (GB, 66–67).

Words in subordinate clauses governed by propositional attitudes seem ambiguous or opaque and are unamenable to substitution because they no longer have their customary reference. They have an indirect reference that coincides with their usual sense (GB, 77) i.e., their usual intension, which is tied to a particular characterization or description of the object. In Frege's words, the sense "serves to illuminate only a single aspect of the thing meant" (GB, 58). Because the words no longer refer to the same object, substitution is bound to fail. They are not truth functional. The truth value depends on something other than what is designated by the sign (PMC, 164).

"An object can be determined in different ways, and every one of these ways of determining it can give rise to a special name, and these different names then have different senses; for it is not self-evident that it is the same object which is being determined in different ways," Frege once wrote in an attempt to explain why senses were objective and indispensable (PMC, 80). "It frequently happens," he wrote to Russell, "that different signs designate the same object but are not necessarily interchangeable because they determine the same object in different ways. It could be said that they lead to it from different directions. . . . A special act of recognition is required. Wherever the coincidence of reference is not self-evident, we have a difference in sense" (PMC, 152). "A sign must therefore be connected with something other than its reference, something that can be different for signs with the same designation. . . . The cognitive value therefore does not depend only on the meaning; the sense is just as essential. Without the latter we should have no knowledge at all" (PMC, 164–65).

One concrete example of how the intensions Frege is talking about surface in discourse involving propositional attitudes can be found in President Kim's attempt to uncover tax evaders discussed in chapter 9. It is thought that up to one-fourth of the many billions of dollars held in financial institutions in his country is held in accounts under false names by people who wish to make tax authorities believe that their assets are less than they actually are. So Kim has decreed that all bank accounts must be registered in the owner's true name. Though, logically speaking, two names for the same account holder would be co-designative, the very reason for having accounts under separate names is that the noninterchangeability of the names blocks the tax man's access to the person holding accounts under other names. This guarantee of nonaccessibility to the reference is in fact one of the most common reasons different names are employed to designate the same object. For example we might have:

(1) The tax authorities know that taxpayer x has more than $1,000,000 in the bank.
(2) Taxpayer x also has an additional $500,000 in an account under the false name 'y'.
(3) Since x = y, the tax authorities know that y has more than $1,000,000 in the bank.

By mere manipulation of symbols we have arrived at statement (3), which is clearly false. And without "a special act of recognition" that is where we will remain. Although 'x' and 'y' are both names for the same tax evader, they are not interchangeable because each name is associated with a different sense, with a different way in which the reference is given. And this fact is brought to the fore by the presence of the propositional attitude 'know'.

Though 'x' and 'y' name the same person, 'x' is that person's real name and 'y' is a false name. So connected with the name 'y' is the additional property of being false. It marks the difference between an honest and a dishonest citizen. So 'y' cannot have the same cognitive value as 'x', and even though both signs designate the same person, they will not be interchangeable (which is exactly what the tax evader is hoping) because they determine it in different ways, lead to it from different directions. A special act of recognition is required (PMC, 152). In Frege's words: "The cognitive value therefore does not depend only on the reference; the sense is just as essential. Without the latter we should have no knowledge at all" (PMC, 164–65). In addition to naming the tax evader, 'y' has the property of being false, which distinguishes it ineluctably from 'x'. And it is this property that comes to the fore once we ask what the tax man knows; the truth or falsehood of the conclusion then no longer turns on the fact that 'x' and 'y' are names for the same tax evader, but on the particular senses attached to each name individually. The point of Kim's decree was to make co-designative names like 'x' and 'y' interchangeable as in the normally extensional:

(4) Taxpayer x has more than a $1,000,000 in the bank.
(5) Taxpayer x also has an additional $500,000 in an account under the name 'y'.
(6) Therefore, y has more than $1,000,000 in the bank.

Suppose, however, that after further inquiry the tax authorities discover that 'y' is a false name, and consequently x and y are the same tax evader. Here the existence of different names for the same person is not a mere irrelevant question of form. For the tax authorities, this fact is the very heart of the matter because each is associated with a different way of determining the contents of that particular person's bank accounts. The matter hinges on something other than who is designated by the names. This is just the valuable sort of information it is their job to uncover.

What the Body Thinks

"If we are limning the true and ultimate structure of reality," Quine wrote in §45 of *Word and Object*, "the canonical scheme for us is the austere scheme that knows . . . no propositional attitudes but only the physical constitution and behavior of organisms." In this section I discuss the important role propositional attitude constructions play in the physical constitution and behavior of organisms by providing some examples of how propositional attitudes bring intensional considerations to the fore in purely physicalistic contexts. To illustrate the points I wish to make I will use some problems in medical science, which are certainly paradigms for many other similar problems.

The scientific findings about juvenile-onset diabetes discussed in chapter 6 provide one example. Some American scientists have found that properties of a protein present in cow's milk are almost identical to properties of a protein present on the surface of insulin-producing cells. The immune systems of people afflicted with this disease mistakes the protein present in cows' milk for the one present on the surface of insulin-producing cells and so begins attacking and destroying it. The similarity of the properties fools the body into thinking (in an obviously unmentalistic sense of the word) that this is the protein present on the surface of insulin-producing cells. So in a non-mentalistic sense of the word 'believes,' the body believes that the protein present in cow's milk is the same as the one the surface of insulin-producing cells. And this mistake can lead to blindness, kidney failure and heart disease.

(1) The diabetic ingests y in the form of cow's milk.
(2) The diabetic's body thinks that a certain property of y is a property of x.
(3) The diabetic's body believes that y = x and tries to destroy it.

For the medical researcher, what is primary is the organism's behavior as dictated by the propositional attitudes in (2) and (3), that the organism thinks and believes x is y to be the case whether it is or not. If his or her idea is correct, the disease will not be cured until that problem is attacked.

Other examples in which propositional attitudes bring intensional considerations to the fore involve the principles involved in the substitutivity of organs in transplant operations. Here again it is what the body thinks that counts. It is a matter of substituting an organ having enough properties in common with the defective organ to make the body think the new organ is equivalent to the old one. Suppose a man donates a kidney to his identical twin brother so that:

(1) The recipient's immune system 'thinks' that healthy kidney x is sufficiently like diseased kidney y not to reject x as foreign.

(2) Therefore, x can be substituted for y, though they are not the same.

Once again the propositional attitude confounds extensionalist reasoning by forcing us to focus on the properties that the two organs may or may not have in common—something which is clearly to the patient's advantage.

In Propria Persona

So the intensions Frege discussed in "On Sense and Reference" in connection with propositional attitudes were not, as has so often been contended,[44] created by him to patch up embarrassing holes in an otherwise parsimonious logical project. They were there for logicians to discover just as Columbus discovered the West Indies. For propositional attitudes produce a bifurcation in the reference of the statements they govern and so display intensions which are eclipsed in other forms of discourse. Whereas in other contexts words merely stand for what they name, so that any phrase in which they occur expresses only a relation between their respective contents, intensions may appear at once in propria persona when part of a sentence is combined with a propositional attitude. Then the words in question no longer stand for their ordinary reference but rather for their ordinary intension.

Understood in this way, problems with propositional attitudes will not go away because the logic itself is producing them. They are produced by a logic conceived in the sin of confusing intensions, words and objects. Because the word or words standing for the ordinary intension (or for the linguistic expression itself) may look the same as the word standing for an object, they can be mistakenly identified with the ordinary reference. Thus, perspicuous logical reasoning would require different signs for distinctly different references. As contexts where use and mention have been confused require that we adopt a convention indicating whether we are using a given word to refer to the word itself, rather than its object, so propositional attitudes indicate that we need a convention showing when words are standing for their ordinary intensions. This is not a matter of having two names for the same object, nor of a name having two kinds of meaning. Rather what we have is a single expression that, on the surface, appears to stand for an object amenable to both substitution and quantification but that needs to be distinguished from what may be the same linguistic expression being used to refer to an intension.

On the surface, some propositional attitude contexts appear to behave like contexts where use and mention have been confused in that they are referentially opaque, i.e., they exhibit untoward behavior as regards substitution, and so misbehave in the presence of existential quantifiers. But the problem arises not because someone has fiddled with the reference process in an improper way, thereby thwarting access to the objects we want to put in our theories and quantify over, but because, like the identity statements studied in part one of this book, propositional attitudes force a bifurcation in meaning. The apparent opacity of these and other intensional contexts, as Ruth Barcan Marcus has pointed out, lies in the way logicians like Quine use the terms 'identity', 'true identity', 'equality', and in particular in their attempts to blind themselves and others to differences between identity and weaker forms of equivalence [45] that always obtain in any non-trivial case in which the difference between the signs in an identity statement corresponds to some intensional difference, some difference in the mode of presentation of thing designated (GB, 57).

A Concluding Grammatical Postscript

A look at surface grammar can provide some insight into the logical form of propositional attitudes. A grammarian well-versed in Frege's writings would tell us that, grammatically speaking, propositional attitude contexts express a relation between an independent attitude ascribing clause and a dependent subordinate clause that may or may not be truth functional in another context. These are complex sentences composed of two parts: one part complete in itself and the other in need of supplementation. The part that is complete in itself is called the independent clause, the part in need of supplementation, the dependent clause. The two parts occupy different and unequal positions in the relation.

In propositional attitude ascriptions, a dependent clause has joined forces with an independent clause to make a complete sentence that expresses a complete thought. The propositional attitude ascription itself is typically an independent clause composed of a grammatical subject and a transitive verb. Its relation to a grammatically dependent clause is usually introduced by the word 'that' or some other such device that acts to make an otherwise independent clause grammatically subordinate to the independent clause.[46] By itself, such a subordinate clause cannot be complete, i.e., cannot be an independent, self-sufficient component of the sentence. It might be said to be 'unsaturated'. Only when supplemented by an independent clause can it contribute to expressing a complete thought.

According to our grammarian, this incompleteness and dependency is precisely why propositional attitude contexts are not amenable to extensional treatment and substitution (re. GB, 24–25, 31, 49, 50). What is dependent is opaque, she believes, and will never acquiesce to extensional treatment. "You see," our surface grammar consultant explains, "what is incomplete is intensional! What is subordinate is insubordinate!!"

11

Modalities

Modal logicians vexed Quine by undertaking to expand classical logic to embrace areas of discourse other than those that can be accommodated in the sterile environment secured by the stringent rules of strong extensional calculi. Much to Quine's dismay, these logicians set out to increase the depth and utility of the standard symbolic languages by developing intensional languages capable of investigating epistemic and deontic contexts and of analyzing the many non-extensional statements that figure significantly in the empirical sciences, law, medicine, ethics, politics, and ordinary philosophy, but that have not been adequately studied within the analytic tradition because they complicate matters by failing to meet the rigid standards set for admission into a logical world as stark as Quine's is (M, 5, 8, 76).

Some particularly deep issues in the philosophy of logic began surfacing when Quine began contending that modern modal logic was illegitimate because he thought, as Ruth Barcan Marcus has said, it was conceived in the sin of confusing use and mention (M, 5; WP, 177). Quine's attempt to discredit modal logic by linking it with such confusions stimulated a debate that widened into an important controversy concerning the existence, true nature, and import of the logical phenomena Quine was decrying. These discussions ultimately raised significant questions about the very nature of the logical enterprise as redefined by Frege, Russell, and their successors, for, as Dagfinn Føllesdal has pointed out, if Quine's judgment was to prove conclusive this would have "disastrous consequences,"

among which would be that "any attempt to build up adequate theories of causation, counterfactuals, probability, prefer-
ence, knowledge, belief, action, duty, responsibility, rightness,
goodness, etc. must be given up."[47] However, the debate finally
served to demonstrate the real existence of the very intensional
phenomena Quine would eradicate.

QUINE'S COMPLAINT

As an integral part of his decades-long campaign against modal
and intensional logics, Quine repeatedly drew analogies between the problems he felt tainted modal logic and the difficulties with substitution and quantification that logicians encounter in contexts where use and mention have been confused.
The kind of inference wrecking referential opacity present
where use and mention are confused also sullies modal contexts, he was keen to point out. By obstructing the substitutivity
of identicals so essential to extensional logic and by foiling attempts at quantification, he warned, modally induced referential opacity disturbs the truth functionality of extensional systems and threatens the simplest and most important modes of
inference in logic (WP, 175–76). Modal operators constitute a
"premeditated departure from extensionality" (WP, 162) and,
where present, they block the access to the "clear extensional
ontology" (OR, 152), that his own logic would guarantee. Logicians trafficking in them, Quine contends, willingly flout the
policy of extensionality adhered to by "adequate logics" (WP,
162). Rather than standing by and watching the most basic logical principles fail, Quine has prevailed upon logicians to abide
by the policy of extensionality "adequate logics" obey, and so
to cross over from the messy gray world of irreferentiality into
his bright, clean one with its "crystal-clear identity concept"
(OR, 21) where all singular terms are under logical control and
obey the simplest and commonest principles of inference.

According to Quine, quantified modal logic might preserve substitutivity only by committing itself to "a curiously idealistic ontology which repudiates material objects," "to an ontology which repudiates classes and admits only attributes." Extending modal logic to include quantification theory would have "queer ontological consequences,"[48] he said. And he has conjured up a nightmare vision of what would happen were logicians to cave into the essentialism he is worried would prevail were quantification into modal contexts to be countenanced. Partisans of modal logics would come and litter his barren landscape with their ugly essences, pollute his pure extensional ontology, thus "precipitating an ontological crisis" (FLPV, 158). They would lead logicians out of his logic's beautiful desert and "back into the metaphysical jungle of Aristotelian essentialism" (WP, 176). Any such connivance with essentialism is a terrible prospect for Quine, and he has bid logicians to steer clear of modal logic's tropical disasterland and to pass instead through the strait gate of classical quantification theory, to remain in the hard won metaphysically pure territory conquerable by faithful logicians willingly enforcing a policy of extensional cleansing (WP, 162).

Quine's Riddle about 9
and the Number of the Planets

As part of his protracted campaign to rid logic of referential opacity, Quine challenged modal logicians to solve a particular puzzle about identity, substitutivity, and modality that he believed served to illustrate the point he wanted to make about the affinities between the referential opacity of contexts where use and mention have been confused and the irreferentiality tainting modal contexts. One version of this riddle which he used over and over in his efforts to stump modal logicians is:

(1) Necessarily 9 exceeds 7.

(2) 9 = the number of the planets.

(3) Therefore, necessarily the number of the planets exceeds 7.[49]

Quine considers statements (1) and (2) to be obvious truths. Yet, as he points out, the substitution of 'the number of the planets' for '9' in (3) transforms the obviously true (1) into the obviously false (3). Although, according to him, '9' and 'the number of the planets' stand for the same object, they are not interchangeable salva veritate in contexts governed by modal operators and so stand in flagrant violation of the substitutivity principle so essential to the extensional logic he espouses.

The position of '9' in (1), Quine considered, is not purely referential, and the source of all the trouble must be the talk of necessity which has invalidated the inference otherwise licensed by existential generalization and the principle of substitutivity of identicals (WO, 197). The number of the planets and 9, Quine reasoned, "are the same thing, yet 9 necessarily exceeds 7 whereas the number of the planets only contingently exceeds 7. So . . . necessarily exceeding 7 is no trait of the neutral thing itself, the number, which is the number of the planets as well as 9. And so it is nonsense to say neutrally that there is *something*, *x*, that necessarily exceeds 7" (WP, 183–84).

By applying existential quantification to modal statement (1) in Quine's puzzle, we might come up with:

(4) (∃x) (x necessarily exceeds 7)

Such an eventuality, according to Quine, shows "how a quantifier applied to a modal sentence may lead simply to nonsense" (FLPV, 150), and makes it apparent that "if to a referentially opaque context of a variable we apply a quantifier, with the intention that it govern that variable from outside the referentially opaque context, then what we commonly end up with is unintended sense or nonsense" (FLPV, 148).

In his "Reply to Professor Marcus," Quine challenged champions of quantified modal logic to solve his riddle:

> The only course open to the champion of quantified modal logic is to meet my strictures head on: to argue in the case of 9 and the number of the planets that this number is, of itself and independently of mode of specification, something that necessarily, not contingently, exceeds 7. This means adopting a frankly inegalitarian attitude toward the various ways of specifying the number. One of the determining traits, the succeeding of 8, is counted as a necessary trait of the number. So are any traits that follow from that one, notably the exceeding of 7. Other uniquely determining traits of the number, notably its numbering the planets, are discounted as contingent traits of the number and held not to belie the fact that the number does still necessarily exceed 7.
>
> This is how essentialism comes in: the invidious distinction between some traits of an object as essential to *it* (by whatever name) and other traits of it as accidental (WP, 184).

MARCUS REPLIES TO QUINE'S OBJECTIONS

Founder of quantified modal logic, Ruth Barcan Marcus, rose to defend the quantified modal logic whose evils and "varied sorrows" Quine has broadcasted and whose reputation he has been so intent on tarnishing through disparaging remarks about the illicit way in which it was conceived (M, 5; WO, §41; WP,

158–84). She has been particularly intent on drawing attention to the real logical issues behind the astronomical riddle Quine challenged modal logicians to solve. "I do not intend to claim," she has written, "that modal logic is wholly without sorrows. I do claim that its sorrows are not those that Quine describes, and that modal logic is worthy of defense, for it is useful in connection with many interesting and important questions, such as the analysis of causation, entailment, obligation, and belief statements, to name only a few" (M, 5).

What Quine has for decades damned as being referentially opaque and would dispose of, Marcus has found to be "of enormous interest" and would explore and chart in a systematic and formal manner using the appropriately intensional language (M, 8). Strongly extensional functional calculi prove "inadequate for the dissection of most ordinary types of empirical statement," she has pointed out (M, 5). However, the fact that "interpretations of standard first-order predicate logic fail as vehicles for paraphrase of important segments of discourse . . . does not and should not prevent us from enlarging our artificial languages so that we may deal with larger and larger fragments of ordinary discourse" (M, 76).

Marcus admits to having experienced difficulty appreciating the force of Quine's argument concerning substitution in modal contexts as expressed in his riddle about the number of the planets. The argument, she thought, had been defanged in the 1940s when Arthur Smullyan[50] and Frederic Fitch[51] showed how logical analysis in accordance with Russell's theory of definite descriptions, one of Quine's favorite theories, effectively dispelled the kinds of puzzles about failures of substitutivity and disturbed inference in modal contexts that were the subject of Quine's complaint (M, 3, 10, 36–38, 109, 209, 225).

"Identity and substitutivity converge where there is reference and transparency of context, up to and including modal contexts," Marcus has argued (M, 124). If '9' and 'the number of the planets' are indeed two names for the same thing, she reasons, then they must be intersubstitutable in every context, even modal contexts. If these are not simply proper names for the same object and the statement expresses equivalences that may possibly be false, e.g., the number of the planets may be either more or less than 9, then Quine's example does not express identity, she points out (M, 12).

The problem with Quine's riddle is precisely that 9 and the number of the planets are not identically the same (M, 28). Substitutivity fails in Quine's example, she argues, because "the logical form of an identity sentence flanked by a description (used descriptively) is not given by '$x = y$'. . . . An identity sentence . . . presumes reference, and descriptions need not refer (be satisfied). Further reasons are entailed by the nature of the identity relation itself, which is the relation between an object and an object just in case it is the same object. That an object is the same as itself is not a contingent matter, but that one object uniquely satisfies two sets of properties may well be" (M, 107).

"On the theory of descriptions," she reminds philosophers, "the identity sign is, after analysis, *never* flanked by descriptive phrases. A singular descriptive phrase specifies a set of properties that uniquely characterize an object if there is one. It does not refer directly to that object" (M, 191–92). "A solution of the dilemma . . . ," Marcus reasons, "requires that the equality relation that holds between expressions such as '9' and 'the number of planets' must be distinguished from the equality relation that holds, for example, between the expressions '9' and '$7 + 2$'. This distinction must be that '$7 + 2$' may replace '9' in modal contexts but 'the number of planets' may not" (M, 37).

Russell's theory of definite descriptions proves to be effective in resolving Quine's dilemma because the example he had appealed to in his attempt to stump modal logicians was not in actual fact a case of modally induced opacity. The problem is that the expression 'the number of the planets' is a description, not a name and so is opaque even in strictly extensional contexts. Once disambiguated 'the number of the planets' is no longer blighted by opacity and no longer causes substitution to fail for those who, like Quine, accept the basic notions underlying Russell's theory of definite descriptions.

Quine had apparently allowed himself to be tricked by the surface grammar of natural languages into thinking that the description 'the number of the planets' was a genuine name (M, 117) and that the logical form of a statement of identity flanked by a description could be given by '$x = y$' (M, 107). His riddle plays on an attempt to identify a name and a description, something that easily happens when one follows ordinary language and grammar too closely for there descriptions actually often appear as names.

Quine on Descriptions as "Seeming Names"

"It is a curious fact," Marcus rightly notes, "that Quine, who leaned on the theory of descriptions in 'On What There Is' as a solution to puzzles about nonreferring singular terms, failed to see its effectiveness in dispelling his apparent puzzles about substitutivity in modal contexts" (M, 192, re. FLPV 1–19). For Russell's theory of definite descriptions also proves to be an effective way of meeting Quine's strictures head on because it is completely in keeping with his own convictions regarding identity, the truth of statements and the eliminability of descriptions, and so shows his objections to be inconsistent on his own terms—independently of whether Russell's theory really does disclose the true logical form of statements containing descriptions.

When Quine declares '9 is the number of the planets' to be a statement of identity, by his own theory of identity he is affirming that he is prepared to extend this statement into '9 is the same object as the number of the planets'. When he calls this same statement a true identity, he further affirms that 'the statement thus formed is true if and only if those component terms refer to the same object' (WO, §24). However, according to his own theories, descriptive phrases are only "seeming names," and it is wrong to suppose they demand objective reference (FLPV, 5–8). Moreover, Quine himself has extolled the virtues of analyzing away descriptions (FLPV, 12) and has advocated having variables of quantification which no longer purport to be names (FLPV, 6) bear the burden of objective reference otherwise wrongly put on descriptive phrases. A statement analyzed by Russell's theory of descriptions, he wrote, "ceases to contain any expression which even purports to name the alleged entity . . . , so that the meaningfulness of the statement no longer can be thought to presuppose that there be such an entity" (FLPV, 7).

QUANTIFICATION AND METAPHYSICS

Extricated by Russell's theory of definite descriptions from the superficial charge that she was guilty of perpetrating modally induced irreferentiality, Marcus addressed the deeper reasons why quantification seems to fail in modal contexts. "It appears to me," she wrote, "that at least some of the problems stem from an absence of an adequate, unequivocal, colloquial translation of the operations of quantification" (M, 16). In particular, Quine's objections would stem from his convictions that "existence is what existential quantification expresses" (OR, 97) and to "be assumed as an entity is, purely and simply, to be reckoned as the value of a variable" (FLPV, 13). Such an understanding of quantification, she observes, "may entangle us unnecessarily in ontological perplexities, for if quantification has to do with things and if variables for attributes or classes can be quantified upon, then . . . attributes or classes are things" (M, 16).

Arguing that "there is a genuine question about the appropriateness or even the meaningfulness of supposing that there is an unequivocal connection between the standard interpretation of the quantifiers and any paraphrase in and out of ordinary and philosophical discourse" (M, 80), she began tampering with the theory of quantification Quine has qualified as bold, bright, simple, beautiful, deep, and useful (OR, 113); she began arguing in favor of what has become known as substitutional quantification—a reading of the existential quantifier which frees us of the ontological baggage of Quine's theory (M, 85) and divorces quantifiers from ontological commitment altogether (M, 79).

"The standard semantics *inflates* the meanings of sentences it paraphrases," she observes, "those, for example, that did not *originally* have the existential import they acquire on such a paraphrase" (M, 82, 122). The logical uses of quantification are preserved under the substitutional interpretation (M, 81), but by freeing logical operators from any ontological bias, she argues, one can avoid ontological inflation and dispel apparent anomalies, including the ones associated with quantifying in and out of a wide range of intensional contexts (M, 82, 122). The substitutional interpretation also "permits a rational rethinking of problems connected with identity and substitutivity" (M, 85) and "frees us to explore generality and existential import in all their subtlety" (M, 82). Quine has conceded that the ontological problems or difficulties of modal logic would not arise were quantification to be interpreted in Marcus's way (M, 26–27) and that the "question of ontology wouldn't arise if there were no quantification of the ordinary sort" (M, 27).

With Russell's theory of definite descriptions and substitutional quantification, substitutivity is preserved and the modal logician need no longer traffic in the weird ontology Quine feels so squeamish about. So Marcus is free to confront Quine's metaphysical charge that the only way out for modal logicians is essentialism (M, 30). Quine writes that "quantifying, in the quantificational sense of quantification, into modal contexts in a modal sense of modality" (M, 35) leads to essentialism. He charges, "If one is to quantify into modal contexts and one is to interpret these modal contexts in the ordinary modal way and one is to interpret quantification as quantification, not in some quasi-quantificatory way that puts the truth conditions in terms of substitutions of expressions, then in order to get a coherent interpretation one has to adopt essentialism" (M, 32).

"So the issue is now the specter of essentialism: a sorting of properties as essential or non-essential to objects that have them" (M, 225). The "whole thrust," Marcus observes, "shifts from a concern with motivation, paradoxes, puzzles, and the senselessness of interpretations of modal logic to claims about modal logic's repugnant essentialist commitments" (M, 219). "Even if claims of puzzlement were set aside or resolved, modal logic would still commit us to some undesirable and unacceptable philosophical or ontological or semantical views" (M, 221, 227).

Marcus does not, however, reject essentialism. She neither considers essentialism invidious (M, xiv) nor talk of essential attributes senseless (M, 51). And "while arguing that "modal languages need not commit one to essentialism," she defends essentiality for certain properties (M, xiv, 230). There are some provably essential attributes in Quantified Modal Logic (QML), she acknowledges (M, 51). She explains:

> A sorting of attributes (or properties) as essential or inessential to an object or objects is not wholly a fabrication of metaphysicians. The distinction is frequently *used* by philosophers and nonphilosophers alike without untoward perplexity. Given their vocation, philosophers have also elaborated

such use in prolix ways. Accordingly, to proclaim that any such classification of properties is "senseless" and "indefensible," and leads into a "metaphysical jungle of Aristotelian essentialism" is impetuous. It supposes that cases of use that appear coherent can be shown not to be so or, alternatively, that there is an analysis that dispels the distinction and does not rely on equally odious notions (M, 54).

"Aristotle seems to me correct," she writes, "when he says that the 'essence' (in the sense of essential properties) of a particular comprises those properties that it shares with all of that species and does not serve to distinguish further among particulars of the species" (M, 231).

Being gold or being a human being is not accidental. . . . No metaphysical mysteries. Such essences are dispositional properties of a very special kind: if an object had such a property and ceased to have it, it would have ceased to exist or it would have changed into something else. If by bombardment a sample of gold was transmuted into lead, its structure would have been so altered and the causal connections between its transient properties that previously obtained would so have changed, that we would not reidentify it as the same thing (M, 69).

"Essentialist talk is frequently unproblematic," she maintains (M, 67). "Modal logic," she affirms, "accommodates essentialist talk. But such talk is commonplace in and out of philosophy. It is surely dubious whether essentialist talk can be replaced by nonessentialist, less 'problematic' discourse" (M, 55).

12

Conclusion

In his 1968 *Leçons sur la première philosophie de Russell*, Jules Vuillemin wrote that Russell had often been considered an iconoclast but that the royal road of metaphysics goes by way of such forms of destruction.[52]

Twentieth century thought has been thoroughly iconoclastic. The icons it earmarked for destruction were variously judged to be fake, outmoded, irrelevant, worn out, meaningless, repulsive, inhibiting, repressive, pernicious, destructive, dangerous, misleading, unproductive, and so on. And in many cases they were. There was a rage to break them, and along with them, the civilization and traditions many people felt they would rather do without.

Figuring among the icons of logic and philosophy marked for demolition were the essences, attributes, senses, meanings, essential properties, attributes, concepts, propositions, and universals of pretwentieth century logic. These were lumped together into one category and branded intensional. According to this new meaning of the old word 'intension', intensions were weird objects. They were a big nuisance, and, worse than that, frustrated and fettered scientific progress. Intensions were demonized and villified. For they raised upsetting questions about the real efficacity of a brave new logic which it was hoped might wipe them out with the stroke of a pen. Many of those who wished to destroy them did not care to grapple with the problems intensions raised or to consider whether recourse to them might actually be necessary, appropriate, right, better, or even simpler, more elegant, more effective, or more efficient.

But intensions did not docilely submit to the logical measures designed to wipe them out or to make them into bizarre entities by deforming them beyond all recognition. For when not given their due, intensions rebel and make their existence known in telling ways which demonstrate their reality and disclose their essential properties. So they survived the campaign to extirpate them, which finally served to demonstrate the reality and ireradicability of what it was trying to remove from philosophical reasoning.

The prominent role Frege accorded identity and substitutivity in his theories makes them superb guides for going about the modern logical world and seeing exactly what is there and how it might be connected with extra-logical reality. Intensions, after all, are notoriously ill-mannered when it comes to substitutivity. So in this study of twentieth century attempts to create a purely extensional ontology, I have invited readers to engage in rationally rethinking certain problems connected with identity and substitutivity in the logic and philosophy that developed out of Frege's ideas.

Arithmetic was the point of departure for the ideas that led Frege to develop his symbolic logic. His symbolic language was modeled after the language of arithmetic, and he first applied his ideas to arithmetic, hoping thereby to arrive at a more detailed analysis of its concepts and a deeper foundation for its theorems. However, Frege's interests were by no means limited to arithmetic. He hoped that his symbolic language might find a broader application and that it might eventually "become a useful tool for the philosopher" (preface to the *Begriffsschrift*).

According to Frege's theory of arithmetic, with numbers it was "a matter of fixing the sense of an identity" (FA, x, §§62, 106). His aim, he said, was "to construct the content of a judgement which can be taken as an identity such that each side of it is a number" (FA, §63). For him, numbers were always independent objects that as such were qualified to figure in identity statements. And he believed that any appearance to the contrary could "always be got around" because expressions which in everyday discourse that did not seem to name independent objects could be rewritten so that they did. As often as not, Frege chose non-arithmetical examples to illustrate the points he wished to make. In this case, he chose the following statements as examples:

(1) 'Jupiter has four moons'
(2) 'Columbus is the discoverer of America'

which, according to his logical ideas, might be reformulated to read:

(3) 'The number of Jupiter's moons = four'
(4) 'Columbus = the discoverer of America'

Here Frege has put the predicative parts of statements (1) and (2) into statements (3) and (4), which he considers to be identity statements in which the descriptions name independent objects. According to his theory, (3) "is an identity, stating that the expression 'the number of Jupiter's moons signifies the same object as the word 'four'." Likewise, in (4) 'Columbus' signifies the same object as 'the discoverer of America' (FA, §57).

Frege's next step in providing a deeper foundation for the theorems of arithmetic consisted in adopting "a means for arriving at that which is to be regarded as being identical" (FA, §63). To this end he appropriated Leibniz's principle that "things are the same as each other, of which one can be substituted for the other without loss of truth" (FA, §65). Here, too, Frege would advocate rephrasing statements in ways that made distinctions obtaining in ordinary language vanish. In this case, he adjusted Leibniz's principle to meet his own ends by translating sentences of natural languages into his symbolic language in a way he thought did away with the differences between being identical (the same in all respects) and being equal (the same in a particular respect). This adjustment, he argued, was in keeping with the way identity was really used in arithmetic.

To achieve his goals he appealed to a process of logical abstraction by which statements in which certain objects are said to be equivalent in terms of a certain property predicated of them are transformed into statements affirming the identity-equality of abstract objects formed out of those properties. In the *Foundations of Arithmetic* Frege used the following examples to illustrate his move:

(5) 'The segments are equal in length'
(6) 'The surfaces are equal in color'

which he wished to see reformulated as

(7) 'The lengths of the segments are equal'
(8) 'The color of the surfaces is equal'.

Here, Frege has changed the statements of sameness of concrete properties predicated of concrete objects in (5) and (6) into statements (7) and (8), which affirm the equality-identity of abstract objects, in this case, surfaces and lengths. He believes he has thus transformed statements about objects that are equal under a certain description into statements expressing a complete identity. Once again, he has rephrased expressions that in everyday discourse did not seem to name independent objects in a way which presupposed that those expressions did name objects; he has accorded the predicative portion of the sentence object status by using constructions containing the definite article 'the', just as he did in (3). And he again has capitalized on ambiguities inherent in the notion of identity to achieve his ends.

But Frege quickly saw that this way of transforming statements of equality into identities engendered new problems. He realized that the procedure was liable to produce nonsensical conclusions, because it only afforded logicians a means of recognizing an object as given in a particular way but did not account for all the ways in which it could be determined. So, he realized, it was liable to be sterile and unproductive because it led to the "obvious" and "sterile" conclusion that all "identities would then amount simply to this, that whatever is given to us in the same way is to be reckoned as the same" (FA, §§66–67). Either the predicates marking the difference between identity and equality really do vanish through logical abstraction (however improbable that may seem), in which case we have only empty tautologies, or the predicative knowledge that serves to make his identity statements informative has slipped somewhere into reasoning where it might yield unexpected results in the form of nonsense or contradictions. For it is no mere matter of form when two expressions having the same reference, but determining it in different ways, are linked together to make a true identity statement. If the identity statement is informative, it is the very heart of the matter.

Seeing that stronger measures were needed to overcome the nonsense or sterility that the removal of properties marking the differences between equality and true identity easily entails, Frege sought relief from his problems by appealing to extensions of concepts or classes. The extension of a concept, he suggested, might go proxy for the concept in identity statements; predicative concept-words would correspond to the expression 'the extension of . . .'. Here again, he was lending object status to something essentially predicative in nature by using expressions with 'the' which he thought named objects because they contained the definite article. Frege was again trying to solve an identity problem and once again ambiguities in the notion of identity that made his attempt seem feasible.

By the time *Basic Laws of Arithmetic I* appeared in 1893, Frege had managed to quiet the reservations he would later confess having had about introducing extensions. Extensions were accorded a fundamental role in that book where he defined number itself as the extension of a concept and laid down Basic Law V to mandate the view of equality his system required. In his most confident moments Frege believed that his law could bring logicians out of what he called the "queer twilight" of identity in which he saw mathematicians performing their logical conjuring tricks.

But when informed of Russell's paradox of the class of all classes that are not members of themselves several years later, Frege designated the logical transformations legitimized by Basic Law V as being the source of the problem, a conviction he retained until the end of his life. The procedure he had hoped would bring identity out of the penumbra into the clear light of day had actually authorized various illicit logical moves that yielded contradictory results by letting logicians put their symbols to wrong uses by allowing type ambiguities to creep into reasoning unnoticed, with the result that, for example, a class might seem to be a member of itself.

Russell set out to discover how and why Frege's theories had given rise to contradiction, and he came up with several specific theories as to the causes of the paradoxes and ways of avoiding them. He first thought the "key to the whole mystery" would be found in restoring the logical structure eclipsed when normally predicative parts of language are treated as if they named independent entities in identity statements in Frege's new way. However important it was to distinguish between logical types, though, Russell later realized that that could not be *the* key to the whole mystery. For the theories of types he would propose treated just the symptoms of a deeper problem.

To solve the whole mystery, Russell would have to understand how and why the type structure had broken down in the first place. In trying to find that out, he progressively reasoned his way backwards through the steps in Frege's reasoning I have just described until coming back to the logical problems concerning identity and substitutivity that had tempted Frege to introduce classes and a law permitting class to be predicated of its own extension in the first place.

The immediate problem about the classes which are not members of themselves suggested to Russell that the contradiction would not go away as long as classes were treated as independent entities. The contradiction showed, he believed, that one could not generally suppose that objects which all have a certain property form a class that is in some sense a new entity distinct from the objects making it up. Unbridled use of the principle of logical abstraction was producing fake objects, which in turn were causing the worrisome contradictions, he considered.

It was while struggling to get to the bottom of that particular problem that Russell uncovered some parallels existing between the problems that arise when classes are treated as objects and problems which come up when descriptions are treated as names. These analogies plus a new technique he had devised for analyzing away descriptions gave him an idea as to how he might make his problems go away.

One of the problems that had led Frege to appeal to extensions or classes in the first place had, in fact, resurfaced for Russell in the form of puzzles about the logical behavior of descriptions in informative identity statements. If x is identical with y, Russell reasoned, then whatever is true of the one is true of the other, and one can be substituted for the other salva veritate. But, if identity is just a matter of two signs standing for the same object, he realized, it would not then seem to have much importance. Identity statements containing descriptive phrases of the form 'the so-and-so' constituted an obvious exception, however. Such statements were plainly not mere tautologies, he observed, for a "proposition containing a description is not identical with what that proposition becomes when a name is substituted, even if the name names the same object as the description describes" (IMP, 174).

It was in trying to solve this puzzle about substitution and sterile statements of identity that Russell invented his famous technique for analyzing away expressions containing the word 'the'. Descriptions seem on the surface to designate objects, but they do not actually designate any entity and so cannot figure in identity statements as if they do, he concluded. He now considered such phrases containing the word 'the' to be incomplete symbols, and he came up with a way of analyzing them that would make them comply to the same formal rules of identity as symbols that directly represent objects—and do so without adversely affecting the truth value of the statements in which they figure. This new theory for making descriptions disappear proved to be an important breakthrough in his search for relief from the paradoxes, for it provided Russell with a practical model of how he might make classes function as entities without incurring contradictory results.

In addition, Russell came to believe that solving the paradoxes would mean coming to terms with problems with classes caused by the fact that it was "quite self-evident that equivalent propositional functions are often not identical" (PofM, 500). He also realized that the "incomplete symbols which take the place of classes serve the purpose of technically providing something identical in the case of two functions having the same extension" (PM, 187), and that, by playing on certain formal similarities existing between these problems and the puzzles about descriptions, he could use his new method of analyzing away incomplete symbols in a way which preserved the vital contribution classes make while making the symbols for them disappear. He could have his classes and delete them too.

But, Russell realized that incomplete symbols could only obey the same formal rules of identity as symbols referring to objects in so far as "we only consider the *equivalence* of the resulting variable (or constant) values of propositional functions and not their identity" (PM, 83), an observation which again took him one step further back to the old problems with logical abstraction, identity and substitutivity which had obliged Frege to introduce extensions in the first place. Russell came to the conclusion that the "ultimate source" of the contradictions was to be found in the fact that the principle that if x and y are identical, ϕx implies ϕy only holds in each particular case, but cannot be said to hold always.

In this connection, Russell was obliged to tackle yet another problem. For he had realized that if the contradiction producing vicious circles were to be avoided, functions would have to be divided into types, but it was easy to show "that the functions which can take a given argument are of an infinite series of types" (IMP, 190). For mathematics to be possible, though, he believed that it was absolutely necessary to have some method of making statements which was usually equivalent to what we have in mind when inaccurately speaking of 'all properties of x' (PM 166; LK, 80).

Evading this problem, he saw, would require drastic measures. To solve it he proposed the axiom of reducibility which was "equivalent to the assumption that 'any combination or disjunction of predicates is equivalent to a single predicate'" (EA, 250; PA, 58–59), and would provide a way of dealing with any function of a particular argument by means of some formally equivalent function of a particular type. This axiom would yield most of the results which would otherwise require one to resort to the problematical notions of all functions or all properties, and so legitimize the great mass of reasoning apparently dependent on such notions. "By the help of the axiom of reducibility," Russell affirmed, "we find that the usual properties of classes result. For example, two formally equivalent functions determine the same class, and conversely, two functions which determine the same class are formally equivalent" (EA, 248-49).

Russell thought of the axiom of reducibility as a generalized form of Leibniz's principle of the identity of indiscernibles. He believed it had the effect of legitimizing statements of identity based on the notion of having all properties in common and would make his definition of identity as powerful as if he had been able to appeal to the forbidden notion of all functions of x. And he believed that without the axiom or its equivalent we would be compelled to regard identity as indefinable. If it could be true, the axiom would neatly rub out the intensions marking the difference between equality and identity. So with it Russell had finally reasoned himself all the way back to the reasons Frege's theory of identity and substitutivity had made him appeal to extensions in the first place.

In spite of their differences, Frege and Russell came to some very strikingly similar conclusions about the problems connected with the set theoretical paradoxes. Frege always held that predicates were by their very nature incomplete. They were void of meaning in isolation and the words or symbols standing for them were unsaturated, in need of completion. Throughout his life he insisted that predicates were fundamentally different from objects, could not play the role of objects, and could not stand in the same relations objects do. For him, functions and concepts were special cases of predicates.

Russell eventually added descriptions and symbols for classes to Frege's list of incomplete symbols "that have absolutely no meaning whatsoever in isolation" and could be expected to exhibit anomalous behavior when treated as objects. "There are a great many sorts of incomplete symbols in logic," Russell warned "and they are sources of a great deal of confusions and false philosophy, because people get misled by grammar" (LK, 253). He said he could not emphasize sufficiently how much error one gets into metaphysics if one fails to realize that descriptions do not name (LK, 252). He considered the word 'the' to be "a word of very great importance" and said he would give the doctrine of this word if he were dead from the waist down (IMP, 167).

Frege concurred. Like Russell, Frege would ultimately warn of "the fatal tendency of language" to form proper names to which no objects correspond and which threatened "to undermine the reliability of thinking" (PW, 269). He once wrote of "the tendency of language by its use of the definite article to stamp as an object what is a function and hence a non-object" which "proves itself to be the source of inaccurate and expressions and so also of errors of thought" (PW, 273).

When specifically asked about the paradoxes of set theory, Frege explained what he thought the problem to be in terms quite like those Russell used. According to Frege, the "essence of the procedure which leads us into a thicket of contradictions" consisted in regarding the objects falling under F as a whole, as an object designated by the name 'set of Fs', 'extension of 'F'', or 'class of Fs', etc. (PMC, 55). He wrote that the paradoxes of set theory "arise because a concept, e.g. fixed star, is connected with something that is called the set of fixed stars, which appears to be determined by the concept—and determined as an object. I thus think of the objects falling under the concept fixed star combined into a whole, which I construe as an object and designate by a proper name, 'the set of fixed stars'. This transformation of a concept into an object is inadmissible; for the set of fixed stars only seems to be an object; in truth there is no such object at all" (PMC, 54, 55).

"The definite article," he explained, "creates the impression that this phrase is meant to designate an object, or, what amounts to the same thing, that 'the concept *star*' is a proper name, whereas 'concept *star*' is surely a designation of a concept and thus could not be more different from a proper name. The difficulties which this idiosyncrasy of language entangles us in are incalculable" (PW, 270). "From this," Frege wrote, "has arisen the paradoxes of set theory which have dealt the death blow to set theory itself" (PW, 269).

Russell struggled long and hard with ambiguities embedded in statements of identity. And he devised some sharp logical instruments to sweep away the problems that begin accumulating when one violates common sense by trying to equate identity with lesser forms of equivalence. But the problems did not all go away. They surfaced again in debates about confusions of use and mention, names and descriptions, intensions and objects, identity and lesser forms of equivalence that came up when philosophers working on modal logic and intensional logics began investigating and analyzing the many non-extensional statements which figure significantly in the empirical sciences, medicine, ethics, law, engineering, politics ordinary philosophy, but which complicate matters by not conforming to the standards set by strong extensional calculi.

In chapters 10 and 11, I presented two challenges facing those seeking to have a clear extensional ontology. In chapter 10, I examined how propositional attitude contexts display intensions that are eclipsed in other forms of discourse. Like informative identity statements, I argued, they again force the issues about intensions by producing a bifurcation in the meaning of the words which brings the senses of the words to the fore.

Whereas in other contexts words merely stand for what they name, so that any phrase in which they occur expresses a relation between their respective contents, intensions may appear in propria persona when part of a sentence is combined with a propositional attitude. Thus words in subordinate clauses governed by propositional attitudes seem ambiguous or opaque and are unamenable to substitution because they no longer have their customary reference. Instead they have an indirect reference that coincides with their usual sense, their usual intension, which is tied to a particular characterization, a particular description of the objects. These contexts are not truth functional because their truth value depends on something other than the reference of the expressions figuring in them. Because the words no longer refer to objects, substitution is bound to fail. Understood in this way, problems with propositional attitudes will not go away because they are being produced by a logic conceived in the sin of confusing intensions, words, and objects.

In Chapter 11, I turned to issues raised by modal logic. As part of his decades-long campaign against modal and intensional logics, Quine repeatedly drew analogies between the problems he felt tainted modal logic and the difficulties with extensionality, substitutivity, and quantification that logicians encounter in contexts where use and mention have been confused. The kind of inference wrecking referential opacity present where use and mention are confused also muddles modal contexts, he was keen to point out. Modal operators, he charged, are symptoms of a perverse and wanton desire to flaunt rules that "adequate logics" respect. To make his point, he repeatedly confronted modal logicians with a riddle about an identity statement in which the definite description 'the number of the planets' is equated with the number 9, an example reminiscent Frege's problematic Jupiter's moons example.

The problems with propositional attitudes and modal logic,

I have argued, have been misdiagnosed by logicians wanting to hold too fast to Quine's ideas about extensionality. It is no use blaming the propositional attitudes or the modal operators for the failures of substitutivity occurring within their purview. For those failures are logic's way of indicating that one has done something illogical by confusing phenomena belonging to essentially different logical types. The situations rather call for analysis by an appropriately intensional language.

Rather than do that, though, Quine has recommended that logicians not venture beyond the narrow confines that strong extensional calculi set for philosophical reasoning. Fortunately, some philosophers, Jaakko Hintikka and Ruth Barcan Marcus, for instance, have taken a rather bolder attitude than Quine has towards limning the true and ultimate structure of reality and have dared to bring light to some of dark areas of logic where philosophers had been warned not to tread. Their efforts have been instrumental in bringing the deeper issues underlying referential opacity, puzzles, contradictions, and paradoxes haunting logical arguments to the surface. In different ways they have contributed to pulling intensions out of the shadowy netherworld to which they were being consigned and into the light of day.

In the above cursory outline of some of the main arguments of this book, I have highlighted some basic moves Frege made in his attempt to subject reasoning to the requirements of an arithmetical conception of identity. To do so, he prescribed certain logical maneuvers that he thought made non-independent components of sentences amenable to substitution the way independent entities are. Fake objects began slipping into reasoning through identity statements in which he identified descriptions with objects, created abstract objects out of properties, and authorized objects to go proxy for concepts—all moves that tore down the predicative structure of natural language and led to the antinomies, contradictions, puzzles paradoxes, and break-downs the principle of substitutivity of identicals and other basic forms of inference that have arisen in connection with informative identity statements, the set-theoretical paradoxes, propositional attitudes, modal and intensional logics, confusions about use and mention, etc.

Natural languages stand ready to invite us into bewildering mazes, and with them we are notoriously free to engage in all kinds of illusions, fantasies, fictions, lies, etc. So Frege was surely right to want to reveal the true logic hidden behind surface grammar and break the domination of the word over the human spirit by weeding out misconceptions, contradictions, ambiguities, and errors that infect natural languages. And he was certainly right to insist on the inviolable ontological and logical differences existing between signs and objects, between concepts and objects, between intensional senses and extensional meaning, between predicative structures and more self-subsistent entities, etc.

But artificial languages have their traps and fetters, too. They can free thought to enter "regions too abstract for the imagination readily to present to the mind the true relation between the ideas employed" (PM, 2). And with them one can easily lose one's sense of extra-logical reality. They can also imprison thought by trying to force it into a rigid mold. Frege's symbolic logic threatened to undermine the reliability of thinking by dismantling some devices natural languages have that reflect apparently inviolable logical differences and act to safeguard against improper inference and other errors in reasoning. He used identity in a way that ultimately violated the very ontological distinctions he himself was most intent on preserving. For abandoning structures natural languages have for distinguishing between identity and lesser forms of equivalence can free thought to enter a logical house of mirrors where certain essential differences are lost.

Frege lucidly wrote of a queer twilight of identity and alluded to the logical conjuring tricks that might be carried out there. The equals sign has an unusual capacity both to confuse and to clarify. In this study of identity, I have tried to break the domination of certain logical ideas over minds of many philosophers by laying bare certain misconceptions that have arisen through the way Frege used the equals sign in his symbolic language. And I have shown that there is confusion where many thought they had found clarity, and that there is clarity where confusion was thought to prevail.

For the equals sign has both an unusual capacity to confuse and an unusual power to clarify. Failures of the principle of substitutivity of identicals are helpful in spotting confusions caused by conscious or unconscious attempts to identify phenomena of different ontological types. They are one of logic's ways of keeping people from really yielding to illusions of clarity achieved by toying with the equals sign, and they are often the first sign that false identification has been made.

Identity helps in finding intensions, and failures of the principle of substitutivity of identicals can often be a first sign an intension has been found. Intensions can, in turn, clear up reasoning, helping to remove ambiguity and imprecision, to draw fine distinctions that are both germane and indispensable to many scientific undertakings. Intensions convey information and recourse to them may be the very thing needed to bring clarity, unity, continuity and elegance to reasoning.

Intensions are powerful. They cause inference failures when they are expected to behave like objects in identity statements. They have the power to bring about the failure of two of the most basic and important modes of inference: the principle of substitutivity of identicals and the principle of existential generalization. They can turn a tautology into an informative identity statement. And when the valuable new information they may convey slips into reasoning unawares, they can be a source of surprises, antinomies, nonsense, confusion, and contradiction, thus disconcerting those intent upon shoving reasoning into an extensional mold.

Intensions are part of the ultimate furniture of the universe, and in limning the true and ultimate structure of reality intensions must be given their due. They cannot be made just to vanish from reasoning, and it is not as easy as some may wish to take leave of them. Even as philosophers like Quine have battled against them, more and more reasons for believing in them have begun gathering ominously right in the austere world philosophers like him were conquering, colonizing, and intent upon defending. They are there to be found just as Columbus discovered the West Indies.

NOTES

1
Unfettering Reasoning

1. As Frege explained in the preface to the *Begriffsschrift*.
2. Wittgenstein, *Tractatus Logico-Philosophicus*, 17–18.

2
The Equals Sign

3. This is one of Frege's major concerns in his 1892 "On Sense and Reference" anthologized in GB, 56–78, the first and last pages especially.
4. See GB, 22–23, 120–21, 141 n., 159–61, and 210; PMC 141. PW 120–21, 182, and Frege's "Review of Dr. E. Husserl's *Philosophy of Arithmetic*" in Frege's *Collected Papers on Mathematics, Logic and Philosophy*, 200, 204.

3
Confusing Sign and Object Identity Statements

5. Quine, *Mathematical Logic,* §4. Carnap makes many of the same points in his *The Logical Syntax of Language,* 153.
6. Quine, "Autobiography," *The Philosophy of W. V. Quine*, Hahn, and Schilpp, eds., 10.
7. Quine, *Mathematical Logic,* §4.
8. See Ishiguro, *Leibniz's Philosophy of Logic and Language,* 17–43. Quine, "Identity," *Methods of Logic,* §35. WO, §24. FLPV, 139–59.
9. See, for example, Quine's ideas in FLPV, 144–46; 12–19. OR, 91–113. WO, §35. *Methods of Logic,* §37.
10. Quine, *Methods of Logic,* §37.

4
Confusing Names and Descriptions in Identity Statements

11. Russell, "My Mental Development," *The Philosophy of Bertrand Russell*, Schilpp, ed., 13–14. Russell, *My Philosophical Development*, 60–61. EA, 165. LK, 262–66.
12. Russell, *My Philosophical Development*, 49.
13. Russell, *Mysticism and Logic*, 218–19.
14. Ibid.
15. Kilmister, *Russell*, 102, 108, 123, 138. Grattan-Guinness, *Dear Russell-Dear Jourdain*, 70, 90. See Russell's statements as cited in note 11 above. Discussed in depth in chapter 9.
16. Grattan-Guinness, "Bertrand Russell on His Paradox and the Multiplicative Axiom: An Unpublished Letter to Philip Jourdain," 106–07, and *Dear Russell-Dear Jourdain*, 78–79.
17. Russell, *My Philosophical Development*, 49.
18. See Quine's views as discussed in chapter 11.

5
Confusing Concepts and Objects in Identity Statements

19. Frege, *Collected Papers on Mathematics, Logic and Philosophy*, 281–83. GB, 43–50. PMC, 96. PW, 119.
20. Frege, *Collected Papers on Mathematics, Logic and Philosophy*, 283.

6
Equating Equality and Identity

21. See Quine, *Methods of Logic*, §§41, 42. *Mathematical Logic*, §24. "New Foundations for Mathematical Logic," and "Reification of Universals" anthologized in FLPV. See Dummett, *Frege: Philosophy of Mathematics*, 155–79. Rodriguez-Consuerga, *The Mathematical Philosophy of Bertrand Russell*, 124–25, 131–34, 139, 148, 153–75, 189–202.
22. Quine, *Mathematical Logic*, §24 "Abstraction." Also FLPV, 90.
23. Marcus, "Modalities and Intensional Languages," "Essentialism in Modal Logic," "Essential Attribution," "Quantification and Ontology," "Does the Principle of Substitutivity Rest on a Mistake?", "Possibilia and Possible Worlds," "A Backward Look at Quine's Animadversions on Modalities," and other articles anthologized in *Modalities*. "Extensionality,"

Mind, 69, 55–62, and anthologized in *Reference and Modality,* Linsky, ed., 44–51.

24. Marcus, "Extensionality," *Reference and Modality,* Linsky, ed., 47.
25. Ibid.

7

Identity and Frege's Foundations for Arithmetic

26. Frege's preface to *Begriffsschrift* in *From Frege to Gödel,* van Heijenoort, ed., 6, 8.
27. I have had to change the translation that reverses the meanings of the words 'equality' and 'identity'.

8

Russell on the Origins of the Set-theoretical Paradoxes

28. Russell, *My Philosophical Development,* 56. Russell first discussed the contradiction at length in PofM, chapter 10 and appendices A and B.
29. *Georg Cantor Briefe,* "Die Phase des Gedankenaustausches mit Hilbert - Anerkennung der Mengenlehre und die Antinomien," H. Meschkowski, and W. Nilson, eds., 387–464. Dauben, "The Paradoxes and Problems of Post-Cantorian Set Theory," *Georg Cantor, His Mathematics and Philosophy of the Infinite,* chapter 11, 240–71. Kline, *Mathematical Thought from Ancient to Modern Times,* vol. 3, 1003, 1184–85.
30. Rang and Thomas, "Zermelo's Discovery of the Russell Paradox," 15–22. In 1903 Hilbert wrote to Frege that Russell's contradiction was already known to Göttingen mathematicians, that Zermelo had discovered it three or four years earlier, and that he himself had found "even more convincing contradictions as long as four or five years ago" (PMC, 51).
31. Hilbert, "On the Infinite" in *From Frege to Gödel,* van Heijenoort, ed., 375.
32. Russell, *My Philosophical Development,* 157. On the subject, see Garcia-diego, *Bertrand Russell and the Origins of the Set-theoretic 'Paradoxes.'* Rodriguez-Consuerga, *The Mathematical Philosophy of Bertrand Russell: Origins and Development.*
33. See *Recent Essays on Truth and the Liar Paradox,* Martin, ed. Barwise, and Etchemendy, *The Liar: An Essay on Truth and Circularity.* Sainsbury, *Paradoxes.* Tarski, "The Concept of Truth in Formalized Languages," §1. Kilmister, *Russell.*

34. Hylton, *Russell, Idealism and the Emergence of Analytic Philosophy*, 227–28, 286.

35. Wittgenstein once suggested to Russell that he use different kinds of symbols to indicate the differences of logical type. See Wittgenstein, *Letters to Russell, Keynes and Moore*, 19. Cited and discussed in Coffa, *The Semantic Tradition from Kant to Carnap*, 152–53.

9
Russell's Paradoxes and His Theory of Definite Descriptions

36. Russell's 1906 letter to Jourdain cited in Grattan-Guinness's, "Bertrand Russell on His Paradox and the Multiplicative Axiom," 106–07. Russell, "My Mental Development," 13–14. Russell, *My Philosophical Development*, 49, 60. Grattan-Guinness, *Dear Jourdain-Dear Russell, a Commentary on Russell's Logic Based on his Correspondence with Philip Jourdain*, 70, 79–80, 94, and note. Kilmister, *Russell*, 102, 108, 123, 138. Grattan-Guinness, "Preliminary Notes on the Historical Significance of Quantification and the Axioms of Choice in Mathematical Analysis," 475–88.

37. Russell, *My Philosophical Development*, 49.

38. Ibid., 58, 60.

39. Rodriguez-Consuerga, "The Origins of Russell's Theory of Descriptions According to the Unpublished Manuscripts," 99–132.

40. Russell, "Knowledge by Acquaintance and Knowledge by Description," *Mysticism and Logic*, 218–19.

41. Ibid., 217–18.

42. Quine, *Set Theory and Its Logic*, 256.

43. Ibid., 253.

10
Propositional Attitudes

44. For example, by Quine in WO, §32, or Evans, *Varieties of Reference*, 8, 20. I discuss this in my *Word and Object in Husserl, Frege and Russell*, 111–12, 121–23, 186.

45. Marcus, "Extensionality."

46. Sentences can be split up in many ways. And natural languages have a way of putting normally intensional expressions to work as grammatical subjects. Like other intensional phenomena, dependent clauses

can be converted into a grammatical subject, as, for example, in the following cases:

(1) That the earth revolves around the sun is by no means self-evident.
(2) That all men are created equal is not agreed upon by all.

Here the dependent clauses have taken the subject place in the sentence. It is about them that something is being said.

As it turns out, Frege's father was a grammarian. See: Kreiser's "Freges ausserwissenschaftliche Quellen seines logischen Denkens," 219–25.

11
Modalities

47. Føllesdal, "Quine on Modality," 179, also 184.
48. Quine, "The Problem of Interpreting Modal Logic," 43–48.
49. See Quine, "Reference and Modality," FLPV, 139–59. WO, §41; "Three Grades of Modal Development." WP, 158–76. "Reply to Professor Marcus," WP, 177–84. "Modalities and Intensional Languages: Discussion," M, 24–29.
50. Smullyan, "Modality and Description," 31–37. And Marcus's review on 149–50 of the same volume, (reprinted, M, 36–38).
51. Fitch, "The Problem of the Morning Star and the Evening Star," 137–41.

12
Conclusion

52. Vuillemin, *Leçons sur la première philosophie de Russell,* 326.

BIBLIOGRAPHY

Angelelli, Ignacio. "Die Zweideutigkeit von Freges Sinn und
Bedeutung." *Allgemeine Zeitschrift für Philosophie*, 3 (1978), 62–66.
———. "Friends and Opponents of the Substitutivity of Identicals in
the History of Logic." *Studien zu Frege*, Matthias Schirn, ed.,
Stuttgart-Bad Cannstatt: Fromann-Holzboog, 1976, 141–66.
———. *Studies on Gottlob Frege and Traditional Philosophy*, Dordrecht:
Reidel, 1967.
Ayer, Alfred J. *Central Questions of Philosophy*, London: Weidenfeld and
Nicolson, 1973.
———. "The Identity of Indiscernibles." *Philosophical Essays*, London:
Macmillan, 1954, 26–35.
———. *Russell and Moore, the Analytical Heritage*, London:
Macmillan, 1971.
Barwise, Jon, and John Etchemendy. *The Liar: An Essay on Truth and
Circularity*, New York: Oxford University Press, 1987.
Bergmann, Walter. "Russell's Examination of Leibniz Examined."
Philosophy of Science, 23 (1956), 175–203.
Black, Max. "The Identity of Indiscernibles." *Mind*, 61, no. 242.
———. *The Nature of Mathematics*, London: Routledge and Kegan
Paul, 1965.
Blackburn, Simon, and Alan Code. "The Power of Russell's Criticism of
Frege: On Denoting pp. 48–50." *Analysis*, 38 (October 1978), 65–77.
Bouveresse, Jacques. "Frege Critique de Kant." *Revue Internationale de
Philosophie*, 130 (1979), 739–60.
Burge, Tyler. "Buridan and Epistemic Paradox." *Philosophical Studies*, 34,
1 (July 1978), 21–35.
———. "Epistemic Paradox." *Journal of Philosophy*, 81, 5–29.
———. "Frege and the Hierarchy." *Synthese*, 40, no. 2 (February 1979),
265–81.
———. "Frege on Extensions of Concepts from 1884 to 1903." *The
Philosophical Review*, 93, no. 1 (January 1984), 3–34.
———. "The Liar Paradox Tangles and Chains." *Philosophical Studies*, 41
(1982), 353–66.

————. "Semantical Paradox." *Journal of Philosophy*, 76 (1979), 169–98.

————. "Sinning Against Frege." *The Philosophical Review*, 88 (1979), 398–432.

Byrd, Michael. "Part II of *The Principles of Mathematics*." Russell, n.s. 7, no. 1 (Summer 1987), 59–67.

Cantor, Georg. *Georg Cantor Briefe*, H. Meschkowski, and W. Nilson, eds., Berlin: Springer, 1991.

Carnap, Rudolf. "Die Antinomien und die Unvollständigkeit der Mathematik." *Monatsh. Math. Phys.*, 41, 1934.

————. "Autobiography." *The Philosophy of Rudolf Carnap*. La Salle, IL: Open Court, 1963, 3–84.

————. *The Logical Syntax of Language*. London: Routledge and Kegan Paul, 1937.

————. *Meaning and Necessity*. Chicago: University of Chicago Press, 1956 (1947).

Church, Alonzo. "A Comparison of Russell's Resolution of the Semantical Antinomies with That of Tarski." *Journal of Symbolic Logic*, 41 (1976), 747–60.

————. "A Formulation of the Simple Theory of Types." *Journal of Symbolic Logic*, 5 (1940), 56–68.

————. "On Carnap's Analysis of Statements of Assertion and Belief." *Analysis*, 10, 5 (1950), 97–99.

————. "Ontological Commitment." *Journal of Philosophy*, 55 (1958), 101–02.

————. "Review of Quine's 'Notes on existence and necessity.'" *Journal of Symbolic Logic*, 8, no. 2 (June 1943), 45–47.

Clavelin, Maurice. "Elucidation philosophique et 'écriture conceptuelle' dans le *Tractatus*." *Wittgenstein et le problème d'une philosophie de la science*, Paris: CNRS, 1971, 104–12.

Cocchiarella, Nino. "Conceptualism, Ramified Logic, and Nominalized Predicates." *Topoi*, 5 (1986), 75–87.

————. "Conceptual Realism as a Formal Ontology." *Formal Ontology*, R. Poli, and P. Simons, eds., Dordrecht: Kluwer, 1994.

————. "Conceptualism, Realism, and Intensional Logic." *Topoi*, 8 (1989), 15–34.

————. "The Development of the Theory of Logical Types and the Notion of a Logical Subject in Russell's Early Philosophy." *Synthese*, 45 (1980), 71–116.

————. *Logical Investigations of Predication Theory and the Problem of Universals*, Naples: Bibliopolis, 1986.

———. *Logical Studies in Early Analytic Philosophy,* Athens: Ohio University Press, 1987.

———. "Predication versus Membership in the Distinction Between Logic as Language and Logic as Calculus." *Synthese,* (1988), 37–72.

———. "Russell's Theory of Logical Types and the Atomistic Hierarchy of Sentences." *Rereading Russell,* C. Savage, and A. Anderson, eds., *Minnesota Studies in the Philosophy of Science,* 12, Minneapolis: University of Minnesota Press, 1989, 41–62.

Coffa, J. Alberto. "The Humble Origins of Russell's Paradox." *Russell,* 33–34 (1979), 31–37.

———. *The Semantic Tradition From Kant to Carnap,* Cambridge: Cambridge University Press, 1991.

Dauben, Joseph. *Georg Cantor, His Mathematics and Philosophy of the Infinite,* Princeton: Princeton University Press, 1990 (1979).

Davidson, Donald, and Jaakko Hintikka, eds. *Words and Objections,* Dordrecht: Reidel, 1969.

de Rouilhan, Philippe. *Frege: les paradoxes de la représentation,* Paris: Minuit, 1988.

———. "Russell and the Vicious Circle Principle." *Philosophical Studies,* 65 (1992), 169–82.

Donnellan, K. S. "Reference and Definite Descriptions." *The Philosophical Review,* 75 (July), 281–304.

Drause, Theodore. "Liar Syllogisms." *Analysis,* 50 (January 1990), 1–7.

Dummett, Michael. "Frege on Functions: A Reply." *The Philosophical Review,* 64 (1955), 96–107.

———. *Frege: Philosophy of Language.* London: Duckworth, 1981 (1973).

———. *Frege: Philosophy of Mathematics.* Cambridge, MA: Harvard University Press, 1991.

———. *The Interpretation of Frege's Philosophy.* Cambridge, MA: Harvard University Press, 1981.

———. "Note: Frege on Functions." *The Philosophical Review,* 65 (1956), 229–30.

———. *The Origins of Analytical Philosophy,* Cambridge, MA: Harvard University Press, 1994.

———. *Truth and Other Enigmas,* Cambridge, MA: Harvard University Press, 1978.

Etchemendy, John. "Tarski on Truth and Logical Consequence." *Journal of Symbolic Logic,* 53, no. 1 (1988), 51–79.

Evans, Gareth. *Varieties of Reference,* Oxford: Clarendon, 1982.

Field, Hartry. *Realism, Mathematics and Modality*, Oxford: Blackwell, 1989.

Fitch, Frederic. "The Problem of the Morning Star and the Evening Star." *Philosophy of Science*, 16 (1949), 131–41.

———. "Towards Proving the Consistency of *Principia Mathematica*." *Bertrand Russell's Philosophy*, G. Nakhnikan, ed., London: Duckworth, 1974, 1–19.

Føllesdal, Dagfinn. "Quantification into Causal Contexts." *Boston Studies in the Philosophy of Science*, 2, R. Cohen, and M. Wartofsky, eds., New York: Humanities Press, 1965, 263–74.

———. "Quine on Modality." *Words and Objections. Essays on the Work of W. V. Quine*, D. Davidson, and J. Hintikka, eds., Boston: Reidel, 1969.

———. "Comments on Quine, Prawitz, Hintikka and Sandu, and Smith." *Synthese*, 98 (1994), 175–86.

Frege, Gottlob. *Basic Laws of Arithmetic*, Berkeley: University of California Press, 1964 (1893).

———. "*Begriffsschrift*, a Formula Language, Modeled upon That of Arithmetic for Pure Thought." In van Heijenoort's *From Frege to Gödel*, 1967 (1879), 1–82.

———. *Collected Papers on Mathematics, Logic and Philosophy*, Oxford: Blackwell, 1984.

———. *Foundations of Arithmetic*, Oxford: Blackwell, 1986 (1884).

———. *Philosophical and Mathematical Correspondence*, Oxford: Blackwell, 1980.

———. *Posthumous Writings*, Oxford: Blackwell, 1979.

———. *Translations from the Philosophical Writings*, Peter Geach, and Max Black, eds. Oxford: Blackwell, 1980.

Frisch, Joseph C. *Extension and Comprehension in Logic*, New York: Philosophical Library, 1969.

Garciadiego, Alejandro. *Bertrand Russell and the Origins of the Set-theoretic 'Paradoxes,'* Basel: Birkhaüser, 1992.

Geach, Peter. "On Frege's Way Out." *Mind*, 65 (1956), 408–09.

———. "Russell on Denoting." *Analysis*, 38 (October 1978), 204–05.

———. "Russell on Meaning and Denoting." *Analysis*, 19 (1959), 69–72.

Gödel, Kurt. *Collected Works*. Oxford: Oxford University Press, 1990–95.

Grattan-Guinness, Ivor. "Achilles is Still Running." *Transactions of the Charles S. Peirce Society*, 10, no. 1 (Winter 1974), 8–16.

———. "Bertrand Russell on His Paradox and the Multiplicative Axiom: An Unpublished Letter to Philip Jourdain." *Journal of Philosophical Logic*, 1, 103–10.

———. "Bertrand Russell's Logical Manuscripts: An Apprehensive Brief." *History and Philosophy of Logic,* 6 (1985), 53–74.

———. *Dear Russell-Dear Jourdain, a Commentary on Russell's Logic Based on His Correspondence with Philip Jourdain,* London: Duckworth, 1977.

———. "Georg Cantor's Influence on Bertrand Russell." *History and Philosophy of Logic,* 1 (1980), 61–93.

———. "How Bertrand Russell Discovered His Paradox." *Historia Mathematica,* 5 (1978), 127–37.

———. "Notes on the Fate of Logicism from *Principia Mathematica* to Gödel's Incompletability Theorem." *History and Philosophy of Logic,* 5 (1984), 67–78.

———. "Preliminary Notes on the Historical Significance of Quantification and the Axioms of Choice in Mathematical Analysis." *Historia Mathematica,* 2 (1975), 475–88.

———. "The Russell Archives: Some New Light on Russell's Logicism." *The Annals of Science,* 31, no. 5 (1974), 387–406.

———. "Russell's Logical Progress, Some New Light From Manuscript Sources." *Historia Mathematica,* 2 (1975), 489–93.

Griffin, Nicholas. "Russell on the Nature of Logic." *Synthese,* 45, 117–88.

———. *Russell's Idealist Apprenticeship,* Oxford: Clarendon, 1990.

Haack, Susan. *Philosophy of Logics,* Cambridge: Cambridge University Press, 1978.

Haaparanta, Leila, ed. *Mind, Meaning and Mathematics,* Dordrecht: Kluwer, 1994.

Haaparanta, Leila, and J. Hintikka, eds. *Frege Synthesized,* Dordrecht: Reidel, 1986.

Haller, Rudolf, ed. *Jenseits von Sein und Nichtsein: Beiträge zur Meinong Forschung,* Graz: Akademische Druck, 1972.

Hallett, Michael. *Cantorian Set Theory and Limitation of Size,* Oxford: Oxford University Press, 1984.

Hilbert, David. "On the Infinite." In van Heijenoort's *From Frege to Gödel,* 1967 (1925), 367–92.

Hill, Claire Ortiz. *Word and Object in Husserl, Frege and Russell: The Roots of Twentieth Century Philosophy,* Athens: Ohio University Press, 1991.

———. "Frege's Letters." *From Dedekind to Gödel: Essays on the Development of the Foundations of Mathematics,* J. Hintikka, ed., Dordrecht: Kluwer, 1996, 96–118.

————. "Husserl and Frege on Substitutivity." *Mind, Meaning and Mathematics*, Leila Haaparanta, ed., Dordrecht: Kluwer, 1994, 113–40.

Hintikka, Jaakko. "A Hundred Years Later: The Rise and Fall of Frege's Influence in Language Theory." *Synthese*, 59 (1984), 27–49.

————. "Identity, Variables and Impredicative Definitions." *Journal of Symbolic Logic*, 21 (1956), 225–45.

————. "Individuals, Possible Worlds, and Epistemic Logic." *Noûs*, 1 (1967), 33–62.

————. *The Intentions of Intentionality and Other New Models for Modalities*, Dordrecht: Reidel, 1975.

————. *Knowledge and Belief*, Ithaca, NY: Cornell University Press, 1962.

————. *Logic, Language Games and Information. Kantian Themes in the Philosophy of Logic*, Oxford: Clarendon, 1973.

————. *The Method of Analysis, Its Geometrical Origin and General Significance*, Dordrecht: Reidel, 1974.

————. *Models for Modalities*, Dordrecht: Reidel, 1969.

————. "Semantics for Propositional Attitudes." Anthologized in Linsky's *Reference and Modality*, 1971, 145–67.

————. "Vicious Circle Principle and the Paradoxes." *Journal of Symbolic Logic*, 22, no. 3, (September 1957), 245–49.

Hintikka, Jaakko, ed., *From Dedekind to Gödel: Essays on the Development of the Foundations of Mathematics*, Dordrecht: Kluwer, 1996.

Hintikka, Jaakko, and Merrill Hintikka. *The Logic of Epistemology and the Epistemology of Logic*, Dordrecht: Kluwer, 1989.

Hintikka, Jaakko, and D. Davidson, eds. *Words and Objections, Essays on the Work of W. V. Quine*, Boston: Reidel, 1969.

Hintikka, Jaakko, and P. Suppes, eds. *Information and Inference*, Dordrecht: Reidel, 1970.

Husserl, Edmund. *Early Writings in the Philosophy of Logic and Mathematics*, Dordrecht: Kluwer, 1994.

————. *Formal and Transcendental Logic*, The Hague: Martinus Nijhoff, 1969 (1929).

————. *Logical Investigations*, New York: Humanities Press, 1970 (1900–01).

————. *Philosophie der Arithmetik. Mit ergänzenden Texten (1890–1901)*, Dordrecht: Kluwer, 1970.

Hylton, Peter. *Russell, Idealism and the Emergence of Analytic Philosophy*, Oxford: Clarendon Press, 1990.

————. "Russell's Substitutional Theory." *Synthese,* 45 (1980), 1–31.

Ishiguro, Hidé. *Leibniz's Philosophy of Logic and Language,* Cambridge: Cambridge University Press, 1990 (1972).

————. "Wittgenstein and the Theory of Types." *Perspectives on the Philosophy of Wittgenstein,* Cambridge, MA: MIT Press, 1981.

Jackson, Howard. "Frege on Sense-Functions." *Analysis,* 23, no. 4, 84–87.

Jacques, Francis. *Reference et Description: Russell, lecteur de Meinong,* Thèse d'Etat, Université de Paris, Nanterre, 1975.

Jevons, Stanley. *Elementary Lessons in Logic: Deductive and Inductive,* 5th ed., London: Macmillan & Co., 1875.

————. *Principles of Science,* London: Macmillan & Co., 1883 (1873).

Jourdain, Philip. "The Development of the Theories of Mathematical Logic and the Principles of Mathematics." *The Quarterly of Pure and Applied Mathematics,* 48 (1912), 219–315.

————. "The Logical Significance of 'Ockham's Razor.'" *The Monist,* 29 (1919), 450–51.

Kant, Immanuel. *Logic,* New York: Dover, 1988 (1800).

Kaplan, David. "How to Russell a Frege-Church." *The Journal of Philosophy,* 72, 716–29.

————. "Opacity." *W. V. Quine,* Lewis Hahn, and P. Schilpp, eds., La Salle, IL: Open Court, 1986, 229–88.

————. "What Is Russell's Theory of Descriptions." *Bertrand Russell,* D. Pears, ed., Garden City, NJ: Doubleday Anchor, 1972, 277–95.

Kaplan, David, and Richard Montague. "A Paradox Regained." *Notre Dame Journal of Formal Logic,* 1, 3 (July 1960), 79–90.

Kauppi, Raili. *Ueber die Leibnizsche Logik mit besonderer Berücksichtigung des Problems der Intension und der Extension,* Helsinki: Acta Philosophica Fennica, fasc. 12, 1969.

Kerry, Benno. "Ueber Anschauung und ihre psychische Verarbeitung." *Vierteljahrsschrift für wissenschaftliche Philosophie,* articles in volumes 9, 10, 11, 13, 14, 15 published from 1885 to 1891.

Kilmister, C. W. *Russell,* London: Harvester Press, 1984.

Klemke, E. D., ed. *Essays on Bertrand Russell,* Urbana: University of Illinois Press, 1971.

————. *Essays on Frege,* Urbana: University of Illinois Press, 1968.

Kline, Morris. *Mathematical Thought from Ancient to Modern Times,* vol. 3 New York: Oxford University Press, 1972.

Kreiser, Lothar. "Bemerkungen zu einer paradoxien Freges." *Teorie a Metoda,* 4/1, 1972.

————. "Freges ausserwissenschaftliche Quellen seines logischen Denkens." *Logik und Mathematik, Frege-Kolloquium Jena 1993,* Berlin: de Gruyter, 1995, 219–25.

Kripke, Saul. *Naming and Necessity,* Oxford: Blackwell, 1980 (1972).

————. "Outline of a Theory of Truth." *Journal of Philosophy,* 72 (1975), 690–716. Also in R. L. Martin's *Recent Essays.*

Kusch, Martin. *Language as Universal Medium vs. Universal Calculus: A Study in Husserl, Heidegger and Gadamer,* Dordrecht: Kluwer, 1989.

Ladrière, Jean. *Les limites internes des formalismes,* Louvain: Nauwelaerts, 1957.

Lewis, David. *Counterfactuals,* Oxford: Blackwell, 1973.

Linke, Paul. "Gottlob Frege als Philosoph." *Zeitschrift für philosophische Forschung,* 1 (1946–47), 75–99.

Linsky, Leonard. *Names and Descriptions,* Chicago: University of Chicago Press, 1977.

————. *Oblique Contexts,* Chicago: University of Chicago Press, 1983.

Linsky, Leonard, ed. *Reference and Modality,* Oxford: Oxford University Press, 1971.

————. *Semantics and Philosophy of Language,* Urbana: University of Illinois Press, 1952.

Lipps, Hans. *Die Verbindlichkeit der Sprache,* Frankfurt: Klostermann, 1958.

Maddy, Penelope. *Realism in Mathematics,* Oxford: Clarendon, 1990.

Marcus, Ruth Barcan. "A Backward Look at Quine's Animadversions on Modalities." *Perspectives on Quine,* R. Barrett, and R. Gibson, eds., Oxford: Blackwell, 1990, 230–43.

————. "Critical Review of Linsky, *Names and Descriptions.*" *Philosophical Review* (July 1978), 497–504.

————. "Does the Principle of Substitutivity Rest on a Mistake?" *The Logical Enterprise,* New Haven: Yale University Press, 1975, 31–38.

————. "Essential Attribution." *The Journal of Philosophy,* 67, no. 7 (1971), 187–202.

————. "Essentialism in Modal Logic." *Noûs,* 1 (March 1967), 91–96.

————. "Extensionality." *Mind,* 69 (1960), 55–62.

————. "The Identity of Individuals in a Strict Functional Calculus of First Order." *Journal of Symbolic Logic,* 12 (1947), 12–15.

————. "Interpreting Quantification." *Inquiry,* 5, no. 3 (1962), 252–59.

————. "Modalities and Intensional Languages." *Synthese,* 13, 4 (1961), 303–22.

————. *Modalities,* New York: Oxford University Press, 1993.

———. "Possibilia and Possible Worlds." *Grazer Philosophische Studien,* 25/26 (1985-86), 107-33.

Martin, Robert L., ed. *Recent Essays on Truth and the Liar Paradox.* Oxford: Clarendon Press, 1984.

———. *The Paradox of the Liar.* New Haven: Yale University Press, 1970.

McDowell, John. "On the Sense and Reference of a Proper Name." *Mind,* 86 (1977), 159-85.

Modal and Many-Valued Logics. Proceedings of a Colloquium in Helsinki, August 23-26, 1962, *Acta Philosophica Fennica,* fasc. 16, 1963.

Montague, Richard. "Syntactical Treatments of Modality with Corollaries on Reflexion Principles and Finite Axiomatizability." In *Modal and Many-Valued Logics,* as cited above, 153-67.

Moore, Gregory. "The Roots of Russell's Paradox." *Russell,* n.s. 8, nos. 1-2, 1988, 46-56.

Neale, Stephen. *Descriptions.* Cambridge, MA: MIT Press, 1990.

Nelson, Leonard. *Beiträge zur Philosophie der Logik und Mathematik mit einführenden und ergänzenden Bemerkungen von Wilhelm Ackermann, Paul Bernays, David Hilbert.* Frankfurt: Verlag Oeffentliches Leben, 1959.

Nidditch, Paul. "Peano and the Recognition of Frege." *Mind,* 72 (1963), 103-10.

Nietzsche, Friedrich. *Das Philosophenbuch,* Paris: Aubier, 1969.

O'Obriant, W. "Russell on Leibniz." *Studia Leibnitiana,* 11 (1979), 159-222.

Palacios, Leopoldus-Eulogius. "De Habitudine Inversa Inter Comprehensionem et Extensionem Conceptuum." *Laval Theologique Philosophique* (February 1971), 81-87.

Parsons, Charles. "The Liar's Paradox." *Journal of Philosophical Logic,* 3 (1974), 381-412.

Picardi, Eva. "Kerry und Frege über Begriff und Gegenstand." *History and Philosophy of Logic,* 15 (1994), 9-32.

Poincaré, Henri. "Les mathématiques et la logique." *Revue de Métaphysique et de Morale,* vol. 13, 815-35 and vol. 14, 17-34.

Quine, W. V. O. "Autobiography." *The Philosophy of W. V. Quine,* L. Hahn, and P. Schilpp, eds., La Salle, IL: Open Court, 1986, 3-46.

———. *From a Logical Point of View,* New York: Harper & Row, 1961 (1953).

———. *Mathematical Logic.* New York: Norton, 1940.

———. *Methods of Logic.* London: Routledge and Kegan Paul, 1962 (1952).

————. "Notes on Existence and Necessity." *The Journal of Philosophy*, 40 (1943), 113–27.

————. *Ontological Relativity and Other Essays.* New York: Columbia University Press, 1969.

————. "On Frege's Way Out." *Mind*, 64 (1955), 145–59.

————. "The Problem of Interpreting Modal Logic." *Journal of Symbolic Logic*, 12, no. 2 (June 1947), 43–48.

————. "Promoting Extensionality." *Synthese*, 98 (1994), 143–51.

————. "Quantifiers and Propositional Attitudes." *Journal of Philosophy*, 53 (1956), 177–87.

————. "Russell's Ontological Development." *Journal of Philosophy*, 63 (1966), 657–67.

————. "Russell's Theory of Types." In Klemke's *Essays on Russell*, 372–87.

————. *Set Theory and Its Logic,* Cambridge, MA: Harvard University Press, 1969.

————. *Ways of Paradox,* Cambridge, MA: Harvard University Press, 1976.

————. *Word and Object,* Cambridge, MA: M.I.T. Press, 1960.

Ramsey, F. P. *The Foundations of Mathematics,* London: Routledge and Kegan Paul, 1978 (1931).

Rang, Bernard, and W. Thomas. "Zermelo's Discovery of the Russell Paradox." *Historia Mathematica* 8, no. 1 (February 1981), 15–22.

Resnik, Michael. *Frege and the Philosophy of Mathematics,* Ithaca, NY: Cornell University Press, 1980.

Richards, J. "Pre-'On Denoting' Manuscripts in the Russell Archives." *Russell*, nos. 21–22 (1976), 28–34.

Rodriguez-Consuerga, Francisco. "A Global Viewpoint on Russell's Philosophy," *Diálogos* (1991), 173–86.

————. *The Mathematical Philosophy of Bertrand Russell: Origins and Development,* Bonn: Birkhäuser, 1991.

————. "The Origins of Russell's Theory of Descriptions According to the Unpublished Manuscripts." *Russell*, 9, no. 2 (1989–90), 99–132.

————. "Review of *Antinomies and Paradoxes. Studies in Russell's Early Philosophy,* ed. by I. Winchester and K. Blackwell." *History and Philosophy of Logic*, 11 (1990), 225–30.

Rosado-Haddock, Guillermo. "Los argumentos del antiplatonismo." *Diálogos*, 47 (1986), 151–67.

————. *Exposición crítica de la filosofía de Gottlob Frege,* 1985.

―――. "Husserl's Epistemology of Mathematics and the Foundation of Platonism in Mathematics." *Husserl Studies,* 4 (1987), 81–102.

―――. "Identity Statements in the Semantics of Sense and Reference." *Logique et analyse,* 100 (1982), 399–411.

―――. "Necessita a posteriori e contingenze a priori in Kripke: Alcune note critiche." *Nominazione,* 2 (June 1981), 205–17.

―――. "On Antiplatonism and Its Dogmas" *Diálogos,* 67 (1996), 7–38.

―――. "On Frege's Two Notions of Sense." *History and Philosophy of Logic,* 7 (1986), 31–41.

―――. "Remarks on Sense and Reference in Frege and Husserl." *Kant-Studien,* 73, Heft 4 (December 1982), 425–39.

―――. "Interderivability of Seemingly Unrelated Mathematical Statements and the Philosophy of Mathematics." *Diálogos,* 59 (1992), 121–34.

―――. "Reseña de Jon Barwise y John Etchemendy *The Language of First-Order Logic.*" *Diálogos,* 61 (1993), 195–218.

Rüstow, A. *Der Lügner, Theorie, Geschichte und Auflösung.* Thesis, University of Leipzig, 1910.

Ruffino, Marco Antonio. "The Context Principle and Wittgenstein's Criticism of Russell's Theory of Types." *Synthese,* 98, no. 3 (March 1994), 401–14.

Russell, Bertrand. *A Critical Exposition of the Philosophy of Leibniz,* London: Allen & Unwin, 1949 (1990).

―――. "Descriptions." *Semantics and the Philosophy of Language,* L. Linsky, ed., Urbana: University of Illinois Press, 1952, 95–108.

―――. *Essays on Analysis,* D. Lackey, ed., London: Allen & Unwin, 1973.

―――. *Human Knowledge, Its Scope and Limits,* London: Allen & Unwin, 1948.

―――. *Inquiry into Meaning and Truth,* London: Allen & Unwin, 1940.

―――. *Introduction to Mathematical Philosophy,* London: Allen & Unwin, 1919.

―――. *Logic and Knowledge,* London: Allen & Unwin, 1956.

―――. "Mr. Strawson on Referring." *Mind,* n.s., 66 (1957), 385–89.

―――. "My Mental Development." *The Philosophy of Bertrand Russell,* Paul Schilpp, ed., Evanston, IL: Northwestern University Press, 1944, 3–20.

―――. *My Philosophical Development,* London: Allen & Unwin, 1959.

―――. *Mysticism and Logic,* London: Allen & Unwin, 1986 (1917).

————. *Principia Mathematica to *56*, Cambridge: Cambridge University Press, 2nd ed., 1964 (1927).

————. *Principles of Mathematics*, London: Norton, 1903.

————. *Problems of Philosophy*, Oxford: Oxford University Press, 1967 (1912).

————. "Review of F. P. Ramsey's *Foundations of Mathematics and Other Logical Essays*." *Mind*, n.s. 46, 476–82.

————. *Theory of Knowledge, the 1913 Manuscript*, London: Allen & Unwin, 1984.

Sainsbury, R. M. *Paradoxes*, Cambridge: Cambridge University Press, 1987.

————. *Russell*, London: Routledge and Kegan Paul, 1979.

Salmon, Nathan. *Frege's Puzzle*, Cambridge, MA: MIT Press, 1986.

————. *Reference and Essence*, Princeton: Princeton University Press, 1981.

Schiffer, Stephen. *Remnants of Meaning*, Cambridge, MA: MIT Press, 1989.

Schilpp, Paul, ed. *The Philosophy of Bertrand Russell*, La Salle, IL: Open Court, 1944.

Schoenflies, Arthur. "Ueber die logischen Paradoxien der Mengenlehre." *Jahresbericht der deutschen Mathematiker-Vereinigung*, 15 (January 1906), 19–26.

Searle, John R. "Russell's Objections to Frege's Theory of Sense and Reference." *Analysis*, 18 (1957), 137–43.

Simons, Peter. "Functional Operations in Frege's *Begriffsschrift*." *History and Philosophy of Logic*, 9 (1988), 35–42.

————. "Who's Afraid of Higher Order Logic?" *Grazer Philosophische Studien*, 44 (1993), 253–64.

————. "Why Is There So Little Sense in *Grundgesetze?*" *Mind*, 101, no. 4 (October 1992).

Skyrms, Brian. "Intensional Aspects of Semantical Self-Reference." *Recent Essays on Truth and the Liar Paradox*, Oxford: Clarendon, 1984, 119–31.

Sluga, Hans. "Frege und die Typentheorie." *Logik und Logikkalkül*, M. Kasbauer, and F. von Kutschera eds., Freiburg, 1962, 195–209.

————. *Gottlob Frege* London: Routledge and Kegan Paul, 1980.

Smith, Barry. "On the Origins of Analytic Philosophy." *Grazer Philosophische Studien*, 35 (1989), 153–73.

————. "Logic and Formal Ontology." *Husserl: a Textbook*, J. N.

Mohanty, and W. Mc Kenna, eds., Lanham, MD: University Press of
America, 1988, 31–68.

———. "The Ontogenesis of Mathematical Objects." *Journal of the
British Society for Phenomenology,* 6 (1975), 91–101.

———. "Putting the World Back into Semantics." *Grazer Philosophische
Studien,* 44, 91–111.

———, and H. Burkhardt eds. *Handbook of Metaphysics and Ontology,*
Munich: Philosophia Verlag, 1991.

Smith, David W., and Ronald McIntyre. "Intentionality via Intensions."
Journal of Philosophy, 68, 541–61.

———. *Husserl and Intentionality,* Dordrecht: Reidel, 1982.

Smullyan, Arthur. "Modality and Description." *Journal of Symbolic Logic,*
13 (1948), 31–37.

Stenlund, Sören. *Language and Philosophical Problems,* London:
Routledge, 1990.

Stroll, Avrum. "What Water Is or Back to Thales." *Midwest Studies in
Philosophy,* 14 (1989), 258–74.

Structure, Method and Meaning, Essays in Honor of H. M. Sheffer, New
York: Liberal Arts Press, 1951.

Studien zu Frege, Matthias Schirn, ed., Stuttgart-Bad Cannstatt:
Frommann-Holzboog, 1976.

Sylvan, Richard Routley. "Radical Pluralism — An Alternative to
Realism, Anti-Realism and Relativism." *Relativism and Realism in
Science,* Dordrecht: Kluwer, 253–91.

Tarski, Alfred. "The Concept of Truth in Formalized Languages." *Logic,
Semantics, Meta-mathematics,* Indianapolis: Hackett, 1983 (1956),
152–278.

———. "The Semantic Conception of Truth." *Philosophy and
Phenomenological Research,* 4 (1944), 341–76.

Thiel, Christian, ed. *Erkenntnistheoretische Grundlagen der Mathematik,*
Hildesheim: Gerstenberg, 1982.

Tichy, Pavel. *The Foundations of Frege's Logic,* Berlin: de Gruyter, 1988.

Tiles, Mary. *The Philosophy of Set Theory,* Oxford: Blackwell, 1989.

Turing, Alan. "Practical Forms of Type Theory." *Journal of Symbolic Logic*
13 (1948), 80–94.

———. "The Reform of Mathematical Notation." Unpublished
manuscript in the Turing Archives at King's College Cambridge.

———. and M. H. A. Newman. "A Formal Theorem in Church's
Theory of Types." *Journal of Symbolic Logic,* 7 (1942), 28–33.

Twardowski, Kasimir. *Zur Lehre vom Inhalt und Gegenstand der Vorstellungen*, Munich: Philosophia Verlag, 1982 (1894).

Van Fraassen, Bas. "Presupposition, Implication and Self-Reference." *The Journal of Philosophy*, 65, 5 (1968), 136–52.

Van Heijenoort, Jean, ed. *From Frege to Gödel*, Cambridge, MA: Harvard, 1967.

———. *Selected Essays*, Naples: Bilbiopolis, 1985.

Vuillemin, Jules. *De la logique à la théologie*, Paris: Flammarion, 1969.

———. "L'élimination des descriptions définies par abstraction chez Frege." *Revue Philosophique*, 156 (1966), 19–40.

———. *Leçons sur la première philosophie de Russell*, Paris: Colin, 1968.

Wade-Savage, C., and Anthony Anderson, eds. *Rereading Russell: Essays in Bertrand Russell's Metaphysics and Epistemology*, Minneapolis: University of Minnesota Press, 1989.

Wang, Hao. *Beyond Analytic Philosophy*, Cambridge, MA: MIT Press, 1986.

———. *From Mathematics to Philosophy*. London: Routledge and Kegan Paul, 1974.

———. *Reflections on Kurt Gödel*. Cambridge, MA: MIT Press, 1987.

Weingartner, Paul. "Die Fraglichkeit der Extensionalitätsthese und die Probleme einer intensionalen Logik." *Jenseits von Sein und Nichtsein*, R. Haller, ed., Graz: Akademische Druck, 1972.

Weyl, Hermann. "Der Circulus vitiosus in der heutigen Begründung der Mathematik." *Jahresberichte der deutscher Mathematiker-Vereinigung* 28 (1919), 85–92.

———. "Ueber die neue Grundlagenkrise der Mathematik." *Math. Zeitschrift*, 20 (1924), 131–50.

Wiggins, David. *Sameness and Substance*, Oxford: Blackwell, 1980.

———. "The Sense and Reference of Predicates: A Running Repair to Frege's Doctrine and a Plea for the Copula." *Frege: Tradition and Influence*, Crispin Wright, ed., Oxford: Blackwell, 1984, 126–43.

Winchester, I., and K. Blackwell, eds. *Antinomies and Paradoxes, Studies in Russell's Early Philosophy*, Hamilton, Ontario: MacMaster University Library Press, 1989.

Wittgenstein, Ludwig. "Notes Dictated to G.E. Moore in Norway," Appendix 2 of *Ludwig Wittgenstein: Notebooks 1914–16*, 2nd ed., Oxford: Blackwell, 1979.

———. *Tractatus Logico-Philosophicus*, London: Routledge and Kegan Paul, 1922.

―――. *Letters to Russell, Keynes and Moore,* G. H. von Wright, and
     G. E. M. Anscombe, eds., New York: Harper & Row, 1961.
Wright, Crispin, ed. *Gottlob Frege: Tradition and Influence,* Oxford:
     Blackwell, 1984.
Yablo, Stephen. "Identity, Essence, and Indiscernibility." *The Journal of
     Philosophy,* 84, no. 6 (June 1987), 293-314.
Zalta, Edward. *Abstract Objects: An Introduction to Axiomatic Metaphysics,*
     Dordrecht: Reidel, 1983.
―――. *Intensional Logic and the Metaphysics of Intentionality,*
     Cambridge, MA: MIT Press, 1988.
Zermelo, Ernst. "Memorandum of a Verbal Communication from
     Zermelo to Husserl." In Husserl's *Early Writings in the Philosophy of
     Logic and Mathematics,* 442.

Index